10-18-73

Frontiers for the Church Today

Frontiers
for the
Church Today

Robert McAfee Brown

New York Oxford University Press 1973

Grateful acknowledgment is made to the following publisher
for permission to quote from *Letters and Papers from Prison*
(Revised, enlarged edition) by Dietrich Bonhoeffer
(Copyright © 1953, 1967, 1971 by SCM Press, Ltd.).

1770620

To the members of the
First Presbyterian Church, Palo Alto, California,
who by their concern to discover new
frontiers for the church
have challenged all my stereotypes about
upper middle-class bourgeois suburban Protestantism

and

to the members of the
Stanford University faculty
who by their concern for
the whole family of man
have challenged all my stereotypes about
Christians having a corner on love of neighbor

this book is dedicated
with
gratitude and affection

Foreword

THE ALUMNI ASSOCIATION and the Board of Trustees of the Austin Presbyterian Theological Seminary established a lectureship in 1945 to bring to the seminary campus some distinguished scholar each year to address an annual midwinter convocation of ministers, students and lay people on some phase of Christian thought.

The Thomas White Currie Bible Class of Highland Park Presbyterian Church of Dallas, Texas, in 1950, undertook the maintenance of this lectureship in memory of the late Dr. Thomas White Currie, founder of the class and president of the seminary from 1921 to 1943.

The series of lectures on this foundation for the year 1966 is included in this volume.

David L. Stitt
PRESIDENT

Austin Presbyterian Theological Seminary
Austin, Texas

Acknowledgments

As noted in the preface, the initial catalyst for this book was an invitation to give the Thomas White Currie Lectures at Austin Theological Seminary, in January 1966, and I owe a great debt to President David Stitt, and others who endured the first draft, for their helpful reactions. The original five lectures were updated and given in April 1968 as the Spring Lectures at the Lexington Theological Seminary and, once more updated, at the Princeton Seminary Summer Institute of Theology, in July 1969. Three groups of laymen heard the series, at the Isle of Shoals Conference off the coast of Maine, at the First Presbyterian Church, Auburn, Alabama, and at the Ecumenical Lay School, Palo Alto, California. Portions of the material were presented to seminarians at Union Theological Seminary, Richmond, Virginia, in the spring of 1968, and at Union Theological Seminary, New York, New York, at the Ash Wednesday Retreat, in 1972. The chapters on images for frontier life, as well as those on revolution and liturgy, were presented to a conference of church musicians at Montreat, North Carolina, in the summer of 1972, and much of the material formed the basis of talks given at the 75th anniversary of the founding of the Presbyterian Church of Southern Africa, Durban, in September 1972. Chapters 2 and 5 have had the benefit of review by members of the West Coast Theological Society.

For all the typing, and for much incidental editorial help, I am indebted to the incomparable quartet that has kept the Religious Studies program going at Stanford: Ruth Headley, Crissy Cherry, Nancy Hill, and Monica Moore.

I have not been able to satisfy all my critics, but I have attempted to listen to them all, and the profit to me has been great.

Preface

> Better something doubtful or over-bold, and therefore
> in need of forgiveness, than nothing at all . . . .
> —Karl Barth, *Church Dogmatics,* IV/3,2, p. 780

While writing this book, I have had one picture firmly before me. It comes from that fount of theological wisdom, *The New Yorker.* A cleric is seated before a typewriter late at night. There is a blank sheet of paper in his typewriter and an equally blank expression on his face. The topic to which he is devoting his energies is "The Role of the Church in a Changing World." The cartoon is an effective safeguard against quick ecclesiastical answers.

In an age when books like this one are likely to draw the comment, "*Another* book on the crisis of the church?" an author had better make clear why he presumes to add to an overdiscussed topic. My response is simple: in presenting this material to a variety of lay and ministerial groups, I have found that it has evoked sufficient response, and even excitement, to justify making it available in printed form. This is no tribute to my insight, but it is a tribute to the insight of those whose ideas I have tried to translate and communicate. I have discovered that much exciting thinking goes on in the upper echelons of Protestantism and Catholicism, but that most of it remains within those upper echelons and seldom makes its way down to what are affectionately, if sometimes condescendingly, known as "the grassroots." This book is my attempt to be the middleman in that important and neglected transaction.

When the invitation to give the Thomas White Currie Lectures at Austin Theological Seminary in January 1966 was first extended, it was my hunch that the time was ripe for a substantial volume on "the doctrine of the church." The hunch was wrong. The interval since that time has not been one of synthesis, but of extraordinary upheaval in the life of the church. This is not the time for theological consolidation in ecclesiology; it is, however, a time for note-taking, note-gathering, and note-sharing, so that others may explore further, attack roundly, or discard immediately. Out of the present ferment about the church new light will emerge, but that time is not yet. So the present volume does not presume to be a "definitive work"; it does presume to offer some ideas that may extend discussion about the nature of the church and the place of the church in the modern world.

I believe in the church. I also believe that the church's severest critics must be those who live within it. I believe that the church is in trouble and that although the gates of hell cannot finally prevail against it, I also believe that human indifference and perversity within its walls can come close. So what follows is in part (to paraphrase Robert Frost) a lover's quarrel with the church, but it is also (to quote Robert Frost directly) "a lover's quarrel with the world," undertaken in the belief that the church does not exist for itself but for the sake of the world. A concern about some of the members of the church family is simultaneously a concern about all the members of the human family, whether they ever darken the door of a church building or not.

It remains only to indicate briefly why I have adopted the imagery of the frontier, beyond the obvious reason that the material was originally prepared for a Texas audience. I believe that the most persistent enemies of the church today are those who are unwilling to move in new directions and adapt to new circumstances, those who rely heavily on the *status quo,* and those who yearn for the old days when it was all so much simpler. A frontier situation, however, challenges all of the old stabilities. To survive on the frontier means to be adaptable and mobile—adaptable to new situations, and mobile to enter into yet newer situations.

The style of life on the frontier is defined in part by what one *brings to* the frontier situation. A flesh and blood pioneer living on the frontier had better be clear how he got there, why he came, and what his reasons are for staying or moving on. But frontier life is also defined by *response to* the specific frontier on which

one finds oneself. If there is no spring, one digs a well. If there is
no ford to cross a river, one builds a bridge. If one has neighbors
who are in need, one offers help. What one does is determined in
large part by one's environment. Though one will bring important
qualities to the situation—ingenuity, determination, the collective memory of other frontier experiments—it will be a disaster
if the collective memory leads only to the repetition in a new
frontier situation of responses appropriate to some other frontier
situation.

The point is obvious. The church in our day is called to live out
a frontier existence. It must cope not with one frontier but with
many, and confront them simultaneously. Different frontiers call
for different postures and different understandings; what is
needed at one time and place must be rejected in another time
and place. Most situations to be met will be neither tidy nor glori-
ous. But this need not be cause for despair. Tidiness is not the
first requisite of frontier life, and glory will only be seen retro-
spectively as a by-product that can never be directly sought.

I recently visited the new Roman Catholic cathedral in San
Francisco. I went reluctantly, because I felt that it should never
have been built in the first place, this being a time, as John Mackay
once said, "for campaign tents rather than cathedrals." However,
I will now confess that the cathedral does symbolize an important relationship of church and world. The modern exterior is
striking (even though unkind critics have compared its shape to
the agitator of a Maytag washer). The interior has a soaring ceil-
ing with small but lovely stained glass windows converging at
the center, and over the altar is a huge *baldacchino*, made of hundreds of pieces of silvered metal that shimmer and sway with the
slightest breath of air and communicate life and vibrancy. All the
proper upward and aspiring sentiments are evoked.

What saves the building from being only upward and aspiring,
and therefore a symbol of retreat from the world, is that all
around the base of the building, at eye level, are gigantic windows
of clear glass; there is a horizontal as well as a vertical pull. Not
virgins, saints, or martyrs here; here, only the rough, cruel lines
of the city, eminently visible and everlastingly present through
the clear glass. Here, cheek by jowl with the soaring lines of
beauty, are the realities of apartment house, parking lot, court-
room, theater, and (monstrosity to end all monstrosities) the Jack

Tar Hotel. There is no way to shut the city out. It is as hauntingly present within the cathedral as without. One does not escape the world by "going to church." One only confronts the world more than before.

So be it. Now and forevermore.

R. M. B.

Heath, Massachusetts
August, 1972

Contents

Frontiers for the Church Today

1

The Penitential Presupposition

> There are few themes so tiresome and profitless as
> bewailing the decline of the churches.
>   —E. Wickham,
>   *Church and People in an Industrial Society*

> It is time for judgment to begin at the house of God.
>   —1 Peter 4:17

Bishop Wickham is right. But so is the author of 1 Peter. Books attacking the church are available in great number. Often they do little more than attack. This book attempts to do more. We will take a brief look at what is wrong with the church, not to wallow in guilt or enjoy strenuous polemic, but as a necessary preparation for staking out frontier areas that require the attention of the church today.

Listening to the outsiders

Where do we start, in finding out what is amiss in the church today? Any conclusion will be arbitrary, but it ought to be clear. We will not start with Holy Scripture, or with Calvin, or with the latest expression of dismay from the pen of a contemporary theologian. We will start with the world to which the church is supposed to minister, a world that has become remarkably disenchanted with the church. We will start, in other words, not by proclaiming but by listening. If God loved the world enough to send Jesus Christ into it, we ought to love the world enough to listen to it for a while, before we confidently claim to have a message for it. Before we offer answers, we need to know the questions.

Helmut Thielicke, whom no one will accuse of having abandoned theology to the latest cultural whim, makes the rather surprising comment:

> No one would deny that there is not a single theologian since the Reformation who can hold a candle to [Schleiermacher] for depth, systematizing power, and continuing influence. Why? Because he did not simply go on spinning old threads and threshing empty straw, but rather *found his questions in a living dialogue with his time,* and out of this polarity there came to him ideas which in many different variations are still our own problems.[1]

Thielicke is right. The methodology employed by Schleiermacher, of engaging in "a living dialogue with his time," is an essential methodology for the church today, particularly when we want to find out what is wrong with the church.

The same willingness to listen has emerged in Roman Catholic theology. The Second Vatican Council, in its pastoral constitution on "The Church and the Modern World," put it this way:

> The church has always had the duty of scrutinizing the signs of the times and of interpreting them in the light of the gospel. Thus, in language intelligible to each generation, she can respond to the perennial questions which men ask about this present life and the life to come, and about the relationship of the one to the other. *We must therefore recognize and understand the world in which we live, its expectations, its longings and its often dramatic characteristics.*[2]

It is to those outside the church that an inquisitive ear must be cocked, so that those inside the church can enter into a living dialogue with the world around them and begin once more to "hear the voice of God in the voice of the times."

When we do listen, what do we hear about the sickness of the church? In all the clamor at least three indictments emerge. They may seem contradictory rather than complementary, but at least they are cumulative, and we will not have done justice

---

[1] H. Thielicke, *The Trouble with the Church* (New York: Harper & Row, 1965), p. 28, italics added.

[2] Cited in W. M. Abbott, ed., *The Documents of Vatican II* (New York: Association Press, 1966), pp. 201-202, italics added.

to what can be heard "from the outside" until we hear at least the following three things.

The trouble with not being in trouble

The most surprising thing about the indictment is the lack of hostility. In America, at least, there is not the strident anti-clericalism or anti-ecclesiasticism that has been the stock-in-trade for centuries in European countries. Nor are there militant atheist groups trying to destroy the church, convinced that only when its pernicious influence has been obliterated will people be truly free. The problem, on the contrary, is one of complete apathy. Those not in the church simply do not care, whereas those who have left the church have done so less in anger than in boredom.

Two brief quotations encapsulate the mood of this first level of indictment. One is Robert Barrat's description of what happens to nominally baptized and confirmed Catholics in France: "They leave the church," he writes, "on tiptoe." There is no angry revolt, just a quiet exit. Nor is this new. The real danger to the church lies in what Barrat calls "the silent hemorrhage which has not stopped draining her lifeblood for several centuries." [3] So churchmen leave the church on tiptoe.

The other quotation is Pierre Berton's summary comment on why he left the Anglican Church. "Mine," he writes, "was a rebellion born of apathy." [4] There could be no more searing indictment of what men have done with the legacy of one who came to bring fire to the earth.

Much of the attack-upon-the-church literature turns out to be little more than a series of footnotes on those two devastating comments: the church is "the bland leading the bland"; it is a "non-prophet organization"; it houses "the comfortable pew" (Pierre Berton's less than neutral descriptive term); to invert a phrase from the prophet Amos, it is "an assembly of solemn voices."

To summarize this part of the indictment, the trouble with

---

[3] R. Barrat in *Commonweal* (September 17, 1965), p. 652.
[4] P. Berton, *The Comfortable Pew* (New York: Lippincott, 1965), p. 20.

the church is that the church is not in trouble. It is not on the firing line, where things are happening. It is not concerned with the events of the day. It is on the sidelines. It can be safely written off. It preaches platitudes to a world in need of marching orders.[5]

The culpability of capitulation

If irrelevance is one indictment of the church, another is the feeling among other critics that the church has sold out. It has capitulated. It has become no more than a reflection of the world about it, and a pale reflection at that.

The critics note that the church is usually the last group to take a stand on issues of importance to the whole human family, such as atomic annihilation, the population explosion, super-zealous nationalism, starvation, American irresponsibility in foreign policy, racism. Indeed, its failure to take a stand is in itself a stand, namely a stand that supports the *status quo*. These critics find it hard to fault Bertrand Russell's complaint of many years ago: "The Church is a force for established opinion and resistance to conscientious protest." [6]

This is what makes the outsider so disenchanted; he asks, "Where is the difference between your embodiment of the gospel and the patterns of the rest of mankind? When you finally do take sides, you do so at a time when it has become fashionable to do so. The defense of your own institutional structures appears to be your primary concern, the spreading of the gospel something to be indulged in only after the establishment has been provided for. So you play it safe. The culture around you calls the tune. If the message of early Christianity was 'Love one another,' your message is 'Attend the church of

---

[5] My own experience in this matter, after living for a decade on the campus of a secular university, is that as far as the church is concerned, most people don't care. Among my liberal friends on the faculty, my church membership is tolerated so long as I oppose Ronald Reagan and am morally outraged by Vietnam. Among my conservative friends, the church is a matter of indifference because it does not noticeably disturb their right to maintain the *status quo* by prolonging the nineteenth century as far into the twentieth as those people in Washington will allow.

[6] Cited in P. Berton, *op cit*, p. 89.

your choice.'" The church, in other words, becomes so introverted that it is unable to respond to cries of need. June Callwood, a Canadian journalist, offers devastating imagery:

> [The church] presents a curious sight, like a busy and slightly boring luxury cruise ship, whose passengers are absorbed by status and self-interest while the ocean around them is thick with numb humanity hopelessly clinging to drowning wreckage.[7]

Why has the church capitulated in this fashion? One clear answer comes from the university students who have sensitive consciences but no use for the church. To them, Jesus is "in," even though the church is out. This is not simply because he had long hair, a beard, and wore sandals. It is fundamentally because, in student lingo, "he put his body where his words were." He did not write articles about corruption in high places, he cleansed the temple. He did not have a high-flown theory about laying down one's life for one's friend, he lay down his own life.

The student's query to the church in the light of all this is, "Why don't you follow your leader? Why are you long on words but short on deeds? Why do you talk about love, but remain silent when Vietnamese children are napalmed? Why do you talk about justice but do so little to root out injustice? Why should an institution such as yours expect a hearing, let alone our allegiance?"

What happens to the church that capitulates? It will be gradually destroyed by the forces to which it surrendered. The dust jacket of a book by Henri Perrin, *Priest and Worker* (Holt, Rinehart and Winston), strikingly represents this situation. Inserted in the jaws of a huge plumber's wrench is a crucifix. If the wrench were to be tightened, the crucifix would crumble —distorted, twisted, and finally crushed beyond recognition. And to the extent the church is the body of Christ, the plight of the church today is no less serious. The power of the cross is not easily apparent against the power of the wrench. Most people would put their money on the wrench without thinking twice.

[7] J. Callwood, *Why the Sea Is Boiling Hot* (Toronto: Ryerson Press, 1965), p. 19.

The indictment of illegitimate intrusion

The third and very different indictment, by those who complain that the real trouble with the church is that it is always putting its nose in where it doesn't belong, is that the church tries to be relevant to every issue on the horizon. As long as the church is merely pronouncing lofty generalities about loving the neighbor, such critics do not seem to mind. But let some cleric or some local or national or world council of churches try to translate the love commandment into how one behaves in the voting booth, or into what one's stand should be on poverty or economic aid to underdeveloped nations, and (to employ a precise theological expression) all hell breaks loose. As long as the church is quietly but efficiently supporting the *status quo* these critics say nothing; it is only when vested interests are challenged that the cry goes up, "religion and politics don't mix," and the counter admonition is insisted upon: "The concern of the church is 'spiritual,' its message is the salvation of the individual soul."

Since the following chapters will answer this particular indictment, little more need be said now, except to suggest that if involvement in the affairs of twentieth-century humanity means that the church must pay a price, then that price must be paid. A church that was born out of persecution should not feel too threatened if persecution, however refined, is once again its lot. An earlier generation of ministers was burned at the stake for causing trouble. Today's ministers are fired, not burned. The love commandment does not exist in a vacuum but in society; and to love in societal terms means concern with and involvment in such societal structures as politics.

The acceptance of the indictment

Here, then, are three indictments from the outsider: the church's irrelevance, the church's capitulation, and, on the other side of the ledger, the church's illegitimate intrusion. What can be said to such indictments by the institutional church itself?

The first response of those within the church must be to accept the indictment and make it their own. A Roman Catholic priest recently expanded a familiar formula to read,

Ecclesia semper reformanda ab extrinsico per Spiritum Sanctum, which he then translated, "The Church is always being reformed by the Holy Spirit, sometimes with the help of a swift kick in the pants from the outside." It could indeed be the office of the Holy Spirit to provide just that kind of outside impetus. God has never insisted that truth must come only from within the walls of the church, and churchmen must be willing to hear the word of the Lord to his people being spoken through those who are either unknowing, or perhaps even unwilling, vehicles of that message.[8] Indeed, those within the church should know, with far greater sensitivity than those outside, just how far the church is from fulfilling its high ·calling.

A poignant example of this increased awareness is contained in Monica Furlong's little book, *With Love to the Church.* Miss Furlong, a British journalist who had grown up outside organized religion, was converted as an adult, and, much to the amazement of her secular friends, became a communicant member of the Church of England. Having come to the church from the outside, she was disturbed by the arrogance she found inside, by a feeling on the part of church people that they were somehow "better" than non-church people. In addition to arrogance she found fear:

> The Mothers' Union feels threatened by divorced people, middle-aged clergymen feel threatened by the vigour and potency of the teen-ager, bishops feel threatened by *Honest to God.* What is lacking, what the early church so impressively seems to have had, is the kind of fearlessness which could allow men to explore people and ideas and experiences very different from what they were used to, blissfully confident that they would find Christ there just as surely as they had found him in the garden or on the road to Emmaus.[9]

After her conversion, Miss Furlong goes on, the disillusionment "cut deep."

Not the disillusion of finding that the certainty of con-

---

[8] Cf. the further development of this theme in R. M. Brown, *The Pseudonyms of God* (Philadelphia: Westminster Press, 1972).
[9] M. Furlong, *With Love to the Church* (London: Hodder and Stoughton, 1965), p. 60.

version did not last. . . . Not the disillusion of discovering how hard it is to love, or how *terrifying* evil can be if you challenge it directly. The disillusion I am talking about is the disillusion of discovering that the Church can behave like anti-Christ, that Christians can use their faith as a protection against ever seeing the truth, or against exposing themselves to life in a genuine way at all.[10]

Faced with the frightening possibility that the faith might cause one to see the truth and expose oneself to life in all of its fullness—in both its greatness and its terror—she discovered that the church, rather than encouraging such fulfillment, helped people insulate themselves from it, at the same time trying to maintain an ecclesiastical *status quo* and preoccupied "with its public image at the expense of its private integrity." [11] And so, from this heightened awareness, comes her plea that the church recover the fearlessness of love.

One way that those within the church seek to avoid the problem is by concentrating on the blindness and blandness of the church in the past, without considering how likely it is that blindness and blandness characterize the church in the present. A historical example makes the point. Here is Thomas Chalmers, at the laying of the cornerstone for a Presbyterian Theological College in Edinburgh:

> We leave to others the passions and problems of this world, and nothing will ever be taught, I trust, in any of our [Divinity] Halls, which shall have the remotest tendency to disturb the existing order of things, or to confound the ranks and distinctions which now obtain in Society.[12]

Thomas Chalmers made that statement in 1846; just two years later Karl Marx wrote the *Communist Manifesto*, and it, rather than "what was taught in the [Divinity] Halls," became the word of hope to downtrodden persons in a world where children were working 12 hours a day, 7 days a week, in coal mines run by good Christian gentlemen whose spiritual nurture

[10] *Ibid.* p. 86.
[11] *Ibid.* p. 81
[12] Cited in M. Gibbs and T. R. Morton, *God's Frozen People* (Philadelphia: Westminster Press, 1964), p. 169.

was provided by ministers trained not "to disturb the existing order of things."

A century and a quarter later, we see very clearly how grotesque and wrong that was. But are we always destined to see these things clearly a century and a quarter later? If Karl Marx spoke the prophetic word to the last century—a word the churches should have absorbed and translated into their own idiom—to whom should the churches be listening today to hear the voice of secular prophets? Are not Eldridge Cleaver, Régis Debray, Ché Guevara the ones who bring a voice of hope when the church finds modern ways to avoid disturbing "the existing order of things?"

Those who hear the indictment and try to make it their own must surely wrestle with the problem of whether or not they can remain within the church. Over a century ago Søren Kierkegaard issued a trumpet call to demolish the walls of that nineteenth-century Jericho, the established church of Denmark: "Whoever thou art," Kierkegaard wrote to his fellow Christians, "by ceasing to take part . . . in the public worship of God . . . thou hast constantly one guilt the less, and that a great one: thou dost not take part in treating God as a fool." [13]

That is purposely strident. How much more anguished and therefore potent is this statement by a young German theological student:

We must try to be at one and the same time *for* the church and *against* the church. They alone can serve her faithfully whose consciences are continually exercised as to whether they ought not, for Christ's sake, to leave her.[14]

The important thing in this statement is not the thought of leaving the church; that proposal is scarcely new. The important thing is the thought that one might feel constrained to leave the church "for Christ's sake." This is the added poignancy of the Christian's appropriation of the secular indictment —not dissatisfaction with a sociological institution, but fear that something created by God to carry on the work of Christ may actually have become a betrayer of Christ.

[13] S. Kierkegaard, *Attack Upon Christendom* (Princeton: Princeton University Press, 1944), p. 59.
[14] Cited in A. Vidler, *20th-Century Defenders of the Faith* (London: S.C.M. Press, 1965), p. 112.

This has been the story of the exodus of many priests and nuns from the Roman Catholic church today. They do not hate the church nor have they forsaken Christ; on the contrary they believe in Christ so profoundly that in loyalty to him they feel that they must leave the institution established in his name, since it hides Christ from the world. They look back not in anger, but in profound sorrow. To be forced to choose between Christ and the church, whether one is Protestant or Catholic, is a measure of the betrayal some people feel today.

The penitential presupposition

What, then, is the proper stance? Many have felt constrained to leave the church, believing that fidelity to Christ forces them to do so. In reality, they may be doing much more than simply being faithful to their consciences; they may be forcing those who remain to take more seriously than they would otherwise, the increasingly desperate plight of the church. If things must get worse before they can get better, then such defections may hasten the day of recognition of that plight.[15]

But our present concern is with those who choose to stay— "for Christ's sake"—and work within the church as agents of its reformation. What then? So far it has been suggested that we must accept the indictment and make it our own, in which case it may be far more searing and saddening than the outsider can imagine. An important part of that acceptance will be a kind of institutional *mea culpa*, an acknowledgment of "our fault, our own fault, our own most grievous fault." This is what is meant by the penitential presupposition. Breast-beating, of course, is not enough, and public breast-beating can be an insidious form of pride—pride at one's humility. Nevertheless all else flows from the presupposition of penitence. For the worst kind of sickness, as G. K. Chesterton once wrote, is the sickness of imagining that one is quite well. No one looks for a cure who is not aware of having a disease.

---

[15] I have dealt in more detail with the alternatives of leaving or staying in *The Ecumenical Revolution*, revised and enlarged edition (Garden City: Doubleday, 1969), Chapter 12.

Fortunately, institutional Christianity is becoming aware of the importance of the penitential presupposition. At the formation of the World Council of Churches in 1948, the delegates declared:

> Within our divided churches, there is much which we confess with penitence before the Lord of the Church, for it is in our estrangement from Him that all our sin has its origin. . . . Within our divided churches it is to our shame that we have so often lived in preoccupation with our internal affairs, looking inward upon our own concerns instead of forgetting ourselves in outgoing love and service.[16]

A remarkably similar Roman Catholic presupposition was embodied in Pope Paul's allocution at the beginning of the second session of Vatican II. Speaking to non-Roman Catholic "observers" about the separation of Christians from one another, he said:

> If we are in any way to blame for that separation, we humbly beg God's forgiveness. And we ask pardon too of our brethren who feel themselves to have been injured by us. For our part, we willingly forgive the injuries which the Catholic Church has suffered, and forget the grief endured during the long series of dissensions and separations.[17]

Ecclesia semper reformanda
(the church always being reformed)

But penitence can never be an end in itself. It can never be more than a presupposition for something else, or it too is in error. The task of Christians and of the church is not to wallow in indulgent penitence, but, "forgetting the things that are

[16] Cited in L. Vischer, ed., *A Documentary History of the Faith and Order Movement* (St. Louis: Bethany Press, 1963), p. 80.

[17] In H. Küng, Y. Congar, and D. O'Hanlon, eds., *Council Speeches of Vatican II* (Paramus, N.J.: Paulist Press, 1964), pp. 146-47. Further examples of corporate penitence will be found in *The Ecumenical Revolution*, Chapters 6 and 7.

behind," to "press on . . . ." The way for the church to press on is by embodying, instead of merely repeating, a slogan that should be removed from the realm of sloganeering: *ecclesia semper reformanda,* the church always being reformed, the church always in the process of reformation. At one time this was a Protestant watchword, and the most exciting thing about it today is that it has been appropriated by Roman Catholics. It is the force behind many of the documents of Vatican II and the moves for reform that have come since that event.[18] The Biblical basis for *ecclesia semper reformanda* is, of course, the injunction in 1 Peter, "It is time for judgment to begin at the house of God." This means, as Karl Rahner had put it, that Christians must always live in a state of "permanent dissatisfaction" with the church.

Shortly after World War II a book was published in Britain called *Toward the Conversion of England;* it suggested that a massive evangelizing campaign be launched. Hendrik Kraemer, a Dutch theologian responded:

> Let us frankly say by using the title of a well-known book, the first requirement for the problem of evangelism is not a conversion of England; but a conversion of the Church.[19]

Those who opt to stay within the church do so on the daring assumption that there can be "a conversion of the church," i.e., a "turning about" in a new direction, so that rather than turning away from new demands in a new day, the church can indeed move toward a frontier existence, with all the possibilities and risks that this entails.

---

[18] Cf. especially the writings of H. Küng, *Structures of the Church* (Notre Dame: University of Notre Dame Press, 1968); *The Church* (New York: Sheed and Ward, 1967); and more recently *Infallible? An Inquiry* (New York: Doubleday, 1971).

[19] Cited in H. J. Margull, *Hope in Action* (Philadelphia: Muhlenburg Press, 1962), p. 108.

2

The Frontier of Mission

Graffito in a subway station: Christ is the answer.
Graffito beneath it: What was the question?

Does the church have a "mission" to the world today? Does it
have something to proclaim? Are people asking any of the
questions for which it offers answers?

Many people will acknowledge that there is a place for the
church as a kind of club for "people who like that sort of
thing," but they insist that the church should leave other
people alone, refrain from meddling in their lives, and stop
seeking converts. The church is all right, in other words, so
long as it does not "go missionary."

Within the church today there is ambivalence over "mission." To some, mission is the super-okay word, an instrument
that divides the truly committed from the lukewarm. Others,
however, are rendered uncomfortable by the word, since it con-
jures up, however wrongly, images of missionaries putting
Mother Hubbard dresses on South Sea island natives or frenetic
evangelists assuring nonbelievers that unless they repent they
will burn through eternity.

Both the elitest and the caricaturist versions should be put
aside, however, for mission is central to any historic understanding of the nature of the church, and we must examine
ways in which it might be important today, before we label
it either precious or crude. The word itself is simple enough,
coming from the Latin verb *missio,* meaning "to send" or "to
send forth." It would seem the natural posture of the church to
be sent forth; thus, the church consists of groups of people
"sent forth" to share with others what has happened to them,
and to invite others, if they so choose,   share in it also. That
much would seem unexceptionable.

Uneasiness about mission

And yet, in many quarters of the church today, there is an uneasiness, if not an embarrassment, about mission. Many wonder by what right the church goes forth, and whether it is any longer the proper posture of the church to seek converts or to evangelize. Because this uneasiness is so widespread, it is important to examine some of the reasons for it, reasons that would have been unheard of in an earlier era of the church.

First, much of the uneasiness about mission comes from *an uneasiness about institutional Christianity.* The church is undergoing such an identity crisis that it is not at all clear that it has a message to proclaim to those outside, or even that, if such a message exists, it is congruent with what the message was in the past. Sometimes, indeed, the institution itself seems to be antithetical to the message it proclaims. It is this, as we saw in the last chapter, that has been at least partly responsible for the great exodus of thousands of Roman Catholic priests and nuns, along with an untold number of Protestant ministers, who have felt that they must leave their church, since their church seemed either irrelevant or insincere. Rather than freeing people for a new kind of creative life in the world, the church seems to stifle the possibility of creativity. To remain in the church, some feel, would be to support a caricature of the original Christian message.[1] With such uncertainty, how can a message be proclaimed or embodied?

A second source of uneasiness about mission centers on the *uneasiness about the exclusivist claims of traditional Christianity.* As long as Christians firmly believed that Christianity was the one true faith, the one way to salvation, the one possibility for men to know God, they were zealous in plucking brands from the burning and enrolling sinners in the one organization that could guarantee eternal salvation. But it is difficult if not impossible today to affirm the old adage, "outside the church there is no salvation," particularly in a world where such a claim would consign most people to damnation. Today's Christians are less confident about equating "salva-

---

[1] For varying treatments of this theme from a Roman Catholic perspective, compare C. Davis, *A Question of Conscience* (New York: Harper & Row, 1967); and G. Baum, The *Credibility of the Church Today* (New York: Herder and Herder, 1968).

tion" with "membership in the church," and recognition that Christians have no sure knowledge about the ultimate destiny of their fellowmen is on the upswing. Increasing numbers of Christians today simply cannot affirm that non-Christians won't make it or that they can produce no good works in their lives or that they must surely be in deep despair (if they only knew it), since they do not possess the good news. Conversely, there are too many "good pagans" at work in the world whose zeal to love their neighbor in need leaves Christians far behind, for Christians to make disparaging remarks about the distance they must be from God.

This questioning of the exclusivist claims of traditional Christianity is illustrated with particular force by the relationship of Christianity to Judaism. In recent years Christians have been forced to read Christian history through Jewish eyes and have discovered how brutal has been the treatment of those from whom Christian faith sprang so that, as Father Flannery perceptively puts it, "the pages Jews have memorized have been torn from our histories of the Christian era." [2] To the Christian, the cross is a manifestation of God's love for all of humanity; to the Jew that same cross is a manifestation of man's hatred for some of humanity, since in its name and under its sign Christians have engaged in widespread persecution and forced conversion. Again we see how grotesque it is that salvation should depend on the acceptance of such versions of traditional Christianity. [3]

A third source of uneasiness about mission is based on *a wider uneasiness about the very nature of the Christian faith itself*. We are not only in a time of institutional upheaval, but of theological upheaval as well, in which the very nature of the Christian message is in the process of radical re-examination. Has anything of "the faith once delivered to the saints" survived the eroding acids of modernity? Does obsessive concern for "relevance" lead the church to hop onto every contemporary bandwagon and discover, just a bit too late, that its ultimate destination is a *cul de sac*? But when new modes and approaches are abandoned for a return to the old "solid gospel,"

[2] E. H. Flannery, *The Anguish of the Jews* (New York: Macmillan, 1965), p. xi.
[3] This theme is pursued in greater detail in *The Ecumenical Revolution,* rev. ed. (New York: Doubleday, 1969), Chapter 15.

does this not involve sacrifice of the intellect that appears to be an abdication of concern for truth?

If today, then, the trumpet is blowing with uncertain sound, who shall be summoned to battle? And if the trumpet sound is so uncertain, is it any wonder that missionary concern should be less than fervent? Who enlists recruits for a campaign that is not clearly defined, a campaign the very meaning of which has been rudely challenged from within? Further, why should others respond to claims that seem predestined to deliver less tomorrow than they promised yesterday?

A fourth source of uneasiness about mission is engendered by the relatively recent acceptance throughout the Christian family of *the primacy of religious liberty and the ultimate rights of conscience*. Institutional Christianity has not been notably generous in its approach to such rights in the past, but both the World Council of Churches and Vatican II are now on record with positions long overdue, but positions that nevertheless appear to some to undercut much of the earlier motivation for missionary activity. During the discussion of religious liberty at Vatican II, many conservative bishops saw correctly that if the church were to accept the notion of full religious liberty for non-Catholics, then such acceptance might undermine the traditional views of the church's exclusive corner on truth and the necessity of being in the church to be assured of salvation. Even though it has been a long-held conviction of traditional Catholic theology that the rights of conscience are ultimate, it was another thing to affirm, as Vatican II finally did, that in the contemporary world one's conscience might lead to the embrace of a faith other than the Catholic faith. To say this, in other words, seemed at least on the surface, to lead to religious indifferentism and a concession that "one faith is as good as another." If, then, one's own faith is not unique, why try to propagate it? Why "go forth" to persuade others of its truth? Why not simply let each person believe as he wishes in the light of his own cultural situation and work out ways of cooperating with the variety of faiths operating in the world today? *Mutatis mutandis*, the same problems have been raised for Protestants who used to claim a unique corner on the truth as part of their own proclamation.[4]

[4] For a further treatment of this problem, together with relevant quotations from the World Council of Churches and Vatican Council documents, see *The Ecumenical Revolution*, Chapters 13 and 14.

Christian convictions that speak to all people

The enumerated reasons for uneasiness about mission, though by no means exhaustive, are sufficient to indicate why the notion of mission is ill favored in church life today. They also suggest that in any reassessment of a basis for mission, the element of coercion must be eliminated. Much of the traditional missionary posture since the time of Augustine (or at least the way that posture was apprehended from outside the church) has embodied an apparent zeal to fulfill the Biblical injunction "Compel them to come in" (Luke 14:23). Even if one felt that this still represented the New Testament imperative, the realities of our pluralistic world would make it an unrealistic tactic. The minute we acknowledge, however, that the basic thrust of the Christian message is an attempt to witness to the redeeming quality of *love*, it becomes apparent that love can never be forced upon another but only offered to another.

From this perspective we can suggest certain things about the Christian message that make those who affirm it desire to share it with all people, since what Christians find true and transforming for themselves are realities they believe can be true for others as well. Without attempting a complete list of such qualities, we can indicate enough of them to suggest that the message does have a universal appeal—i.e., an appeal not limited to a handful of the human race but one that can speak healingly and creatively to all. To the degree that such qualities speak to the human situation, a substantial case that Christians can and should share their convictions exists; at the same time the nature of those convictions will preclude the desire to spread them coercively.

One reason for a concern with mission is that Christianity *offers a sense of meaning in a world that seems capricious if not malevolent*. To be sure, other religions offer a sense of meaning at the time that some contemporary ideologies are suggesting that the search for meaning is a fruitless one. Thus, we see a competition between various faiths, which will be won by the faith that makes the most sense out of the most facts in a universe that defies easy explanation. This does not mean reducing life to a series of rational propositions (as the subsequent discussion will indicate) nor reducing the Christian faith to no more than a description of ourselves and our world.

But as we confront a world that frequently seems silent in response to our cry for meaning, there is something worth examining in the Christian claim that love and creativity are clues to an understanding of that world.

How such a claim can be substantiated in the face of much evidence to the contrary is another question. The present point, however, is that any community that accepts such a claim, with all that it would mean for the life of others in the world, surely has no choice but to consider itself "sent forth" in mission, since it has something of utmost importance to share. Such a community is saying (using whatever new terminology is necessary to make the point in the modern world) that what is ultimate is love and that the deepest and highest things people can experience in the name of love are not will-o'-the-wisps, but pointers to ultimate reality. Such a community is saying that there are such pointers within human experience and that they are the best clues available to the meaning and purpose of the human endeavor. These pointers are not intuitions or evanescent dreams, but are rooted within the fabric of human experience—the history of the Jews, the events clustered around the life and death of a particular first-century Jew, the community that arose in response to the effect that one Jew had upon their lives. Here is a point at which life is drawn together and invested with a meaning that makes it possible for persons to live without despair.

The content of this claim is a second reason for a new concern with mission, namely that Christianity *offers a sense of joy in a world of fear.* It is easy to sound sentimental or cheap about such a claim, and superficial "sunny Christians" who have not measured reality in sober terms must be disavowed. But it must also be noted that the message of Christian faith is a message that could be fairly summarized by the exhortation "Fear not!" So fundamental and powerful is this theme that the sense of joy can even be juxtaposed with the reality of suffering without being thereby destroyed. It was said of Jesus, for example, that he was one "who for the joy that was set before him, endured the cross . . ." (Hebrews 12:2). Against the charge that Christianity is sentimental, it must be underlined that the message of joy came out of a historical event that can only be described as denial of joy, namely an ugly, drawn-out execution hard on the heels of a blatant miscarriage of justice. (It is an interesting commentary on the Biblical worldview itself that the message "Fear not!" frequently comes to people on the lips of angelic visitors whose very presence inspired fear—a fact that should dispose once and for all the notion that confrontation with deity is a simple and unthreatening experience.)

To the degree that joy is the content of the Christian message, it is clear that the message is a message for all and not for a few, for joy is diminished and finally destroyed if it is not shared. Joy is not truly understood if it is parochially nourished and dispensed only to those who are "good" church members. The Christian who affirms joy in a world of fear is not denying that fear can be terribly real and potentially destructive, but he is asserting that though it is real it need not be destructive. This joy by its very nature brings the community formed by it to move outward to share its joy with all.

A third reason for a new concern with mission is that Christianity *offers reconciliation in a world divided and estranged*. A significant attempt to restate a concern for mission was made in the Confession of 1967 of the United Presbyterian Church, which focused on the theme of reconciliation. To begin to overcome the forces dividing humanity, our triple alienation—from self, neighbor, and God—must first be recognized.[5]

There is no need to detail the sense of division, estrangement, and alienation in the world today. We see these wherever we look—old vs. young, professor vs. student, male vs. female, Arab vs. Jew, radical vs. liberal, black vs. white. The list is long. There is no one who does not experience estrangement, and there are few for whom the degree of estrangement is not so high as to make almost unbearable the specter of life's destroyed possibilities.

Probably no claim could be made today that would be more important for all people than a claim that in the midst of our

---

[5] When the Confession of 1967 is updated, or a new one written, it will be important to emphasize a fact that has been emerging in this period of ecological concern, namely that we are alienated from nature as well, and that we are called upon to be reconciled not only to self, neighbor, and God, but also to our environment. The consequences of the latter alienation are now coming to be seen as equally threatening to the human future. See Chapter 5.

bent and broken world healing and reconciliation are nevertheless possible. Such a claim would offer that which contemporary humanity most needs. And if anything characterizes the nature of Christian faith, it is the claim that Christianity (however poorly its protagonists have embodied it) can heal the division.

"However poorly its protagonists have embodied it" is not merely a qualification necessitated by a realistic analysis, but an implied suggestion about the way in which the "message" of reconciliation must be communicated. It is a suggestion that the nature of the Christian message is not an easy verbalization, but the embodiment of a transformed existence. The church's message of reconciliation will be "communicated" to the modern world as reconciliation is embodied in its own life, not by any number of statements about the possibility of such reconciliation. To the degree that the church does exemplify "the reconciling and the reconciled community" it will, simply by so being, issue an invitation to men to experience reconciliation themselves. It was Nietzsche's complaint against Christianity that "the redeemed do not look redeemed." In this area, then, the church's task is not to "compel them to come in," but to create a community with the sort of reconciling openness that will draw persons either into it or inspire them to embody a similar kind of reconciliation of their own.

A fourth reason for a new concern for mission is that Christianity *celebrates a sense of mystery in a world we do not understand even after we have "explained" it.* Such an assertion is immediately open to misunderstanding, for it moves with seductive ease into a theology of "the god of the gaps," a god who is useful as existing just beyond the periphery of those things we still don't understand and who will be needed less and less as we understand more and more.

But the reason for invoking a sense of mystery is not to offer a description of "things we don't yet understand," but rather to describe the way we handle the things we do understand. A scientific colleague of mine divides his friends into the "So what?" scientists and the "Gee whiz!" scientists, the former accepting without surprise whatever their research uncovers, the latter perpetually amazed at the intricacy and delicate balance they find in the world they explore, coupled with an ongoing sense of wonder that a solution to one prob-

lem only unveils a fresh mystery somewhere else. The celebration of mystery, in other words, is not a way of talking
about what is still unknown, but *a way of affirming what is
already known, so that we know it in a new way.* Even in a
world of computers, the arts continue. People give expression
to the many dimensions of their existence in ways that are not
reducible to predictable formulas or data-gathering processes
or the amount of a glandular secretion. It is important that a
sense of wonder continue to intrude into and inform all
cultures and all societies, no matter how much people try to
build fences against it.

In this situation, an important contribution of Christian
faith, as Dietrich Bonhoeffer so powerfully pointed out, has
been to insist that mystery is not found at the edges of life
(the "god of the gaps" syndrome) but in the midst of life. In
the Christian story, it focuses in the mystery that a single
human life (that of Jesus of Nazareth) has been the bearer
of a particularly luminous meaning, and in the meaning that
a single human life (that of Jesus of Nazareth) has been the
bearer of a particularly luminous mystery. A faith that offers
some clues about why mystery and wonder remain, and that
acknowledges that this dimension of life is present in the most
commonplace events of life, is indicating that mystery and
wonder can be gateways to the other qualities we have mentioned—reconciliation, joy, and meaning. Once again such a
faith clearly cries out to be shared, since people who confront
the reality of mystery seek ways to be partakers of it.

Let us be clear as to where we have come on this brief
journey. We have not attempted to "prove" that the Christian
faith is true simply because there are universal human needs
and problems to which Christianity responds. We have rather
attempted to show that the nature of the Christian claim is
that it speaks not only to the needs of a few but to the needs
of all, and that to the degree that one accepts the Christian
claim one's concern is therefore a concern for all and not for
a few. This is simply another way of saying that such a faith
is committed to mission. It is a faith that is "sent forth" for
others to examine and then accept or reject what they find
offered to them.

Therefore the church can never settle for cultivating its own garden and concerning itself only with the dwindling number of "'the faithful." What is actually true for some is potentially true for all, and rather than build fences between itself and the rest of the human family, the church must tear down these fences as soon as possible.

3

From the Frontier of Ecumenism to the Frontier of the Secular

Those who ignore history are doomed to repeat it.
—George Santayana

By virtue of the Creation, and, still more, of the Incarnation, nothing here below is profane for those who know how to see.
—Teilhard de Chardin, *The Divine Milieu,* p. 35

William Temple once spoke of the ecumenical movement as "the great new fact of our era." But the statement no longer quickens the ecclesiastical pulse the way it used to. Something has gone wrong.

The "ecumenical doldrums"

We are at a stage in ecumenical history that many are calling "the ecumenical doldrums." The initial excitement has worn off; the old questions about episcopacy or tradition or clergy-laity distinctions seem to be just that: "old." At such a time, a plea to examine our ecumenical past is likely to fail. Nevertheless, it is my thesis that we are at a critical point in the development of ecumenism, and what we can learn from the past will guide us in the future. To return to the nautical image with which we began, when a ship is "in the doldrums," and all forward motion seems to have ceased, those on board must look out for any fresh breath of wind and be willing, if need be, to reset the sails in order to take full advantage of it and continue on course.

We will look at some of the lessons that have been learned from the past half-century of Protestant ecumenical concern, to see how these have been applied to the subsequent Protestant-

Catholic situation, and then suggest that the same lessons are applicable to the still wider situation of Christians (both Protestant and Catholic) in relation to the whole human family. This also illustrates a return to *oikoumene,* the original meaning of which was not initially a theological concept at all but a "secular" one, standing for no more but no less than "the inhabited world." The true ecumenical frontier is thus not the church but the whole world.

Four lessons from Protestant ecumenical history

We can symbolically identify the beginning of current interest in ecumenism with the Edinburgh missionary conference of 1910, at which for the first time world missionary bodies raised the question of working cooperatively rather than divisively.[1] In the subsequent half-century, a great deal of water went over the ecumenical dam, and at least four lessons have been learned that can be applied creatively for the future:

1. The most important of these has been the realization that *we are already one and our task is to manifest that oneness more fully.*[2] It is a misperception to believe that the ecumenical task is to "achieve" unity or oneness. All who confess Christ and have been baptized in his name are already one in him, no matter how well their denominations may have succeeded in hiding that fact. No Christian can say, "Christ is divided; let us put him back together again." All the Christian can say is, "Christ is one and we are one in him, but by our division we have badly obscured that fact both to ourselves and to the world. Let us therefore find ways to overcome those divisions in order to manifest more clearly what is already true about those who are in Christ." So unity is not man's future achievement. It is God's continuing gift.

2. The concern of the nineteenth-century church was to reach out to all corners of the earth and proclaim Christ everywhere. But the church discovered that its concern for outreach, for mission, was seriously blunted by its disunity. How could the

[1] A historical summary of these and other ecumenical currents is contained in the first three chapters of *The Ecumenical Revolution,* rev. ed. (New York: Doubleday, 1969).

[2] On this point cf. *inter alia,* A. C. Outler, *The Christian Tradition and the Unity We Seek* (New York: Oxford University Press, 1957).

church preach Christ as one who draws all people together, when those who preached that message were not themselves drawn together by him? How could the churches justify the exportation to the Orient of a divisiveness that was Occidental, if not accidental? Why should a convert in Hong Kong have to describe herself as "a Canadian Baptist?" Consequently a second conviction emerged: *unity and outreach belong together.* Not only is the ecumenical movement concerned that the church engage in outreach, it is also concerned that the church reaching out be a united church. As far back as 1952 this often-overlooked point was made by the International Missionary Council at Willingen:

> We believe that the unity of the churches is an essential condition of effective witness and advance. In the lands of the younger churches divided witness is a crippling handicap. We of the younger churches feel this very keenly. While unity may be desirable in the lands of the older churches, it is *imperative* to those in the younger churches . . . . We can no longer be content to accept our divisions as normal.[3]

3. Since unity and outreach belong together this means that *our present divisions are both anachronistic and sinful.* It can be granted that denominationalism played an important role in early Protestantism, maintaining certain emphases that might otherwise have been lost. But that situation no longer obtains in contemporary denominationalism. We no longer need Baptists and Congregationalists to guarantee the integrity of the local congregation, Presbyterians to ensure a free pulpit dedicated to expounding the word of God, Methodists to stress personal salvation, or Episcopalians to order the liturgy. Such concerns are now shared; their retention is not dependent upon retention of the denominations that were historically their champions.

Today the multiplicity of denominations obscures rather than clarifies the content of the one faith they all profess to share. This means, candidly, that one of the most important things denominations can do today is to die, acknowledging themselves to be structures that now distort the gospel they

[3] Cited in N. Goodall, ed., *Missions Under the Cross* (New York: Friendship Press, 1953), pp. 38–39.

were called into being to illumine and embody. When we recall that death was the precondition for Christ's resurrection, we have no reason to suppose that the church that describes itself as his body should travel an any less exacting route.

4. It will be some time, however, before denominational death and ecclesiastical resurrection take place. In the meantime, *we must do everything together that our convictions do not compel us to do separately*. The Faith and Order Conference at Lund (1952) made the point by interrogation:

> There are truths about the nature of God and His Church which will remain forever closed to us unless we act together in obedience to the unity which is already ours. We would, therefore, earnestly request our Churches to consider whether they are doing all they ought to do to manifest the oneness of the people of God. Should not our Churches ask themselves whether they are showing sufficient eagerness to enter into conversation with other Churches, *and whether they should not act together in all matters except those in which deep differences of conviction compel them to act separately?* [4]

Lund's complicated interrogative must be turned into a simple declarative sentence. Until quite recently the explicit proposal that we "act together in all matters except those in which deep differences of conviction compel [us] to act separately . . ." has been ignored in favor of the implicit principle that "we act separately in all matters except those in which deep convergences of conviction compel us to act together." There is a crucial difference between the two convictions: one posits division as normal and conceives of common witness as strange, whereas the other posits unity as normal and conceives of divided witness as strange. While the former conviction obtains, the latter conviction is beyond reach.

Applying the lessons to Protestant-Catholic experience

Those four lessons emerged out of a half-century of Protestant ecumenical experience. They were learned in almost total isolation from Roman Catholicism, which looked upon ecumenism

[4] Cited in O. S. Tompkins, ed., *The Third World Conferences on Faith and Order* (London: S.C.M. Press, 1953), p. 16; italics added.

with a somewhat jaundiced eye until the beginning of Pope
John's pontificate in 1959. Since then, doors to the future have
been opened that no one thought could be unlocked, let alone
passed through. A decade and a half of Roman Catholic ecumenical openness has shown that the same four lessons are
almost equally applicable to the Protestant-Catholic scene today:

1. To a far greater degree than was first realized, Protestants and Catholics *are already one, and our task is to manifest
that oneness more fully.* It was not possible before to come
close to saying this. But the ground broken by Vatican II makes
it easier to continue to do so. Both Protestants and Catholics
acknowledge that baptism incorporates one into the body of
Christ, and each group accepts the validity of the baptism of
the other. Each accepts the fact that the other is in some true
sense a "church" even though the notion still sticks in the
throats of a few.[5] The old Catholic description of Protestants
as "*separated* brethren" is now inflected as "separated *brethren,*"
and more and more frequently the adjective is not only de-
emphasized but deleted. Differences remain on such matters
as papacy, episcopacy, and sacraments—not peripheral items,
to be sure—but so rapidly are these concepts being reconceived
in ecumenically sponsored discussion, that considerably before
the eschaton even these questions may come to a satisfactory
ecumenical resolution. The operative assumption, in other
words, is that we are in fact one and that we can find ways to
transcend the present divisions that render our underlying
unity so difficult to discern.

2. Just as divided Protestants discovered that *unity and
outreach belong together* so too have twentieth-century Protestants and Catholics. To a greater degree than most people
realize, this unity is already a reality on the "mission field."
Before Anglo-Saxon Protestants and Catholics could agree on
a common translation of the Bible, Protestant and Catholic
missionaries in the Dutch East Indies had collaborated on a

[5] Vatican II—a long time ago as ecumenical history is written in these
days—moved in successive drafts of the document *On Ecumenism*
from describing Protestants as members of sociological "communities" to the more theological description of their membership in
"*ecclesial* communities" and acknowledged that a good deal of "ecclesial reality" is present in Protestant life. See further, T. F. Stransky,
ed., *The Decree on Ecumenism* (Glen Rock: Paulist Press, 1965).

single translation. In a day when American Catholics and Protestants use the same building for worship only when an existing edifice has burned down, Catholic and Protestant missionaries in Tanzania and many other countries build joint church and school facilities. Where civic cooperation proceeds slowly and hesitantly in more "established" areas, Catholics and Protestants abroad (realizing that their combined membership may represent only three to four per cent of the total population of a country) make a point of working together whenever possible.

If one takes seriously John Wesley's notion (recently restated for Catholics by Father Yves Congar, O.P.) that "the whole world is my parish," then what is happening "over there" sets the pattern for what is going to happen "back here." Unity and outreach belong together. To whatever degree any Christian body has a mission to the world today, that mission must be pursued in conjunction with other Christian bodies.

3. Protestant ecumenism learned that *our present divisions are both anachronistic and sinful* and that denominations must be prepared to die so that the church may live. Certainly it is a presupposition on the Catholic-Protestant scene that our differences are anachronistic and sinful. Are we at the stage where we can urge that our churches must die in order that the Church may live? Such thinking has been foreign to Roman Catholics in the past, for whom the structural realities of the church have been a part of the gospel entrusted to the church. And the tenacity with which Protestant denominations resist reunion proposals is eloquent testimony to the fact that old denominations, unlike old soldiers, not only never die, they do not even fade away.

If it is clear from Protestant theology that such tenacity is misplaced, it is also clear that there are Catholic resources for a fresh look at the problem. More and more Roman Catholics are prepared to say, as Vatican II both said and demonstrated, that the church as we now know it stands in need of constant reform and renewal. Whatever "the coming great Church" of the future is like, it will not be like the Roman Catholic church of the past. However haltingly it has moved since Vatican II, the church is in the midst of an irreversible program of reform and renewal. The language is no longer about the "seamless robe of Christ without spot or wrinkle," but about a pilgrim people on their way to an unknown destination. Past confidence (or fear) that "Rome will never change" is clearly a misplaced confidence (or fear). The pre-Vatican II definition of the Roman Catholic church is dying, and a new vision of the church is coming to birth—a birth that like all births is painful.

4. In the light of these realities, the Lund question likewise must become the post-Lund exortation: Protestants and Catholics must *do everything together that our convictions do not compel us to do separately.* We can already pray together and picket together without compromising our convictions. And even though we cannot yet officially sit together at the Lord's Table, any honest picketing and/or praying Protestant and/or Catholic would admit that those who have engaged in such activities together do not in fact exclude one another from the Lord's Table. *De facto*, the issue of "intercommunion" is scarcely a problem any more, even though it may be some time before bishops and denominational officials become aware of the fact.

The clearest example of "doing things together" is in the area of social concern. On any of the major crisis issues of the past decade—Vietnam, race, poverty, urban deterioration—Catholics and Protestants have increasingly worked together, both domestically and on a world-wide scale. Where such cooperation is lacking it is now actively sought, and few new programs are launched without making sure that the widest possible ecumenical representation has been achieved.

The exciting thing about this area of shared activity is that the progression is geometric rather than arithmetic; each new area of shared experience opens a multitude of further areas in which sharing now seems possible for the first time.

Interlude: Assessing ecumenical fears

There are some, of course, who take no comfort in ecumenical escalation and would like to reverse the process.

For some, ecumenism is a sellout, the end result of a least-common-denominator type of faith, a product of theological and ecclesiastical indifferentism in which the truth is subverted for the sake of good feeling.

The evidence thus far accumulated belies the fear. In the course of its history, the World Council of Churches, for example, has moved toward more rather than less theological precision. The original basis of membership in 1948 was simply the acceptance of "Jesus Christ as God and Saviour." After thirteen years of living together, the constituent bodies amplified rather than diminished that statement in 1961, so that it now includes a scriptural foundation, an explicit trinitarian formulation, and a recognition of the need for witness in the world:

> The World Council of Churches is a fellowship of Churches which confess the Lord Jesus Christ as God and Saviour according to the Scriptures and therefore seek to fulfill their common calling to the glory of the one God, Father, Son, and Holy Spirit.[6]

This does not mean that the end product of ecumenism will be a rigid orthodoxy. Indeed, in sifting through the theological accumulation of many centuries, one tradition may discover in the light of challenges from another tradition that it can jettison much of its theological baggage and learn once again to "travel light." Infallibility will be redefined, as will *sola scriptura*. What will emerge will be a new understanding of those things that are central, whereas things peripheral will be discovered to be just that.

Recent ecumenical advances have also produced a fear of absorption, a fear that one group will swallow up the others. Several years ago a Catholic poster for the Week of Prayer for Christian Unity showed Christians from all over the world streaming into St. Peter's in Rome. If that is the hope of some Catholics, it is surely the fear of many Protestants. The fear of absorption explains why small demonimations hesitate to merge with larger ones, why middle-sized denominations are apprehensive about joining the World Council of Churches, and why large denominations already in the World Council fear the potential membership of the Roman Catholic church in that body.

If the fear is that denominational identity will be lost, the

---

[6] W. A. Visser 't Hooft, ed., *The New Delhi Report* (New York: Association Press, 1961), p. 37.

fear is well founded. But if the fear is that the distinctive gifts of the denomination will be destroyed, ecumenical experience leads to the opposite conclusion. The Church of South India is a case in point. Formed in 1948, it brought together for the first time since the Reformation era churches from episcopal, presbyterian, and congregational polities. In the intervening quarter of a century, no one of these has absorbed the others. On the contrary there has been mutual enrichment. Episcopacy has not destroyed the significance of the presbyter but has enhanced it. Powers given to the congregation have not smothered episcopacy but have helped all to see the relationship between bishop and congregation in new and more dynamic ways. The emerging pattern is that of enrichment, not diminishment of a denomination's contribution.

Another ecumenical fear is that a united church will become a monolith, stifling creativity and ongoing reform, whether the monolith is directed from "Rome," "Geneva," "Constantinople," or "475 Riverside Drive, New York, New York 10027." If the worst fears were realized, and a monolith did result, it would be time for a new reformation. But it is far from clear that ecumenism will develop according to this projection. It is very clear that no one wants a monolith—Catholics because they are just escaping from one, and Protestants because they have always feared becoming one and realize that their own structures are already more monolithic than they like to admit. The key issue here is the conviction that unity does not mean uniformity. All extant plans for church union take this matter into account. Recognition of the danger of a monolithic structure is at least half the battle, and vigilance against new tendencies to over-centralization is a good part of the other half.

From the ecumenical frontier to the secular frontier

Without discounting the importance of intramural ecumenism, we must note that it could become hopelessly introverted if it were not leavened by outside ferment. Indeed in the face of what is going on outside—the struggle against poverty, hunger, war, and racism—much of the intramural activity seems trivial and misplaced and could be likened to rearranging the deck chairs on a sinking ship. But along with the apparent inward-turning has come a corresponding outward-turning, as the concerns of the *oikoumene*, the inhabited world, have increasingly been seen to be the concerns of the church as well. To take seriously a belief that "the church is for the sake of the world" is to be caught up short in any attempt to let "church-existence" be an end in itself and to realize that only as the church is placing world concern above institutional concern is it fulfilling its vocation.

This is in fact the direction which ecumenical energies have increasingly taken, not as a denial of ecumenism, but as its fulfillment. We can thus advance the argument by taking the four lessons learned from past ecumenical history and seeing how they apply to the entire inhabited world, and not only to that part of the inhabited world of church people. In conducting this enterprise we shift our vocabulary slightly, and what we have heretofore referred to as the *oikoumene* we now describe as the "secular," a term more commonly in use and meaning, in its simplest definition "of or pertaining to the world." [7]

1. Just as members of the Christian family discovered that they already shared a basic unity, so the members of the human family have been making the similar discovery that *we are already one and that our task is to manifest that oneness more fully*.[8] Granting all the richness and diversity that is made possible by the contributions of various races, cultures, and nations, it is now seen to be not only a theological belief but a sociological reality that God "has made from one every nation of men to live on all the face of the earth" (Acts 17:26). Our realization of this fact is due not only to, say, a study of the number of human chromosomes; it is also due to the fact that space travel and planetary probes have given us a new sense of perspective about the oneness of our world that makes our unity undeniable.

Two recent images of the world have helped us to appreciate this reality. One is "spaceship earth," first suggested by Ken-

[7] On the theme of the secular, cf. the brief comments in Chapter 4 and the writings of such theologians as Arend van Leeuwen, Harvey Cox, Colin Williams, and Friedrich Gogarten.

[8] This theme, which upon reflection turns out to be far from self-evident, is explored in detail in J. R. Nelson, ed., *No Man Is Alien: Essays on the Unity of Mankind* (Leiden: E. J. Brill, 1971), 334 pp.

neth Boulding and subsequently developed by Barbara Ward and R. Buckminster Fuller.[9] Those on "spaceship earth" must work together or the spaceship will run out of supplies or self-destruct. If we seek to set up private or invincible hegemonies on spaceship earth, denying our unity, we will not in fact make our own situation safer and our power less vulnerable, but will do precisely the opposite: we will render everybody's situation more precarious and our power more subject to challenge and attack.

The second image is Marshall McLuhan's "global village." [10] One need not accept McLuhan's entire position to appreciate the descriptive truth in the image. Humanity has a *de facto* unity that must be expressed more clearly: those within any village must learn to live and work together if they do not wish to be subject to outside attack or internal divisiveness— either of which can destroy them.

2. Those who dwell in the global village, or who maneuver spaceship earth, are increasingly discovering that attempts to improve the situation of the inhabitants have to be done together. The human family is discovering what the Christian family discovered: *unity and outreach belong together.* Since we are one family, we must reach out as one family: a polio vaccine may not be developed only for people with white skin; docking platforms on space stations must have interchangeable Russian, American, and Chinese coupling systems; if every child in North America is to have enough food, it is imperative that every child in South America, India, Asia and Africa have enough also.

The notion that benefits to some of the human family must be shared with all the rest is probably a truism to those who already think globally, but the sad fact is that most of the inhabitants of the global village or spaceship earth still do not think globally; thus, our purview is limited because our past training and experience have left us with divisive per-

[9] Cf. *inter alia,* "The Economics of the Coming Spaceship Earth," reprinted in K. E. Boulding, *Beyond Economics* (Ann Arbor: Ann Arbor Paperbacks, 1970); B. Ward, *Spaceship Earth* (New York: Columbia University Press, 1966); and R. B. Fuller, *Operating Manual for Spaceship Earth* (Carbondale: Southern Illinois University Press, 1969).

[10] Cf. M. McLuhan and Q. Fiore, *War and Peace in the Global Village* (New York: Bantam Books, Inc., 1971).

spectives. This brings us to the third point.

3. Not only do we have divisiveness on spaceship earth and in the global village, but we perpetuate this divisiveness in ways that are reminiscent of ongoing Protestant division and Catholic-Protestant division. What has been true of the churches is also true of the entire human family: *our present divisions are both anachronistic and sinful.* The nation-state is the clearest example of such division, for in the name of the nation-state we extend and reinforce the divisions within the human family. The president of the most powerful nation on earth orders his troops to invade a neutral country, using the most sophisticated weaponry ever devised, and does untold devastation—all for the sake of "national honor." The same nation lands a team of astronauts on the moon and, instead of claiming it for all humanity, ostentatiously plants an American flag on its surface and thus extends a divisive nationalism from a single planet into outer space.

In the age of spaceship earth and the global village, such actions are not only anachronistic, relics of a time in human history now clearly past, they are also sinful, since they perpetuate the very divisiveness that led to wars based on the economic and political imbalances of the past. They must be overcome if mankind is to survive, let alone grow, in the future.

4. The new conviction that must therefore dominate the future of the entire human family is simply an extension of the insight of the Lund Conference: *we must do everything together that our convictions do not compel us to do separately.* We must hope that the inhabitants of spaceship earth and the global village learn to do this more rapidly than church members have done, since much more is at stake. There is surely no kind of scientific research today that "our convictions compel us to do separately." If it is responded that military research on weapons of greater destructiveness must be done nationally, it can be responded in turn that in this age of nuclear overkill the need for such research has been rendered obsolete, and if the researchers cannot find areas to investigate that benefit all of us rather than jeopardize most of us, then the research had better stop. No longer do political decisions have only domestic implications; they have international implications. Hundreds of thousands of Vietnamese would still be alive if there had been an effective deterrent to the unilateral decisions of Presidents

Johnson and Nixon to bomb at will. So interlocked is international trade and so interdependent are people with respect to world markets and access to raw materials, that international agreements in all these areas are not only desirable but absolutely necessary.

One who responds that the extension of the four points noted above is visionary should be reminded that such an extension is mandatory and that it can be demanded on the basis of the most hard-nosed kind of realism. At a time when American division made American unity urgent, Benjamin Franklin stated, "Gentlemen, if we do not hang together, we will all hang separately." We can update his advice by noting that if we do not follow humanity's instinct for unity, humanity will become extinct in disunity.

This, then, is the kind of world in which the church today is placed—a world that is being forced to go in the same directions that the church is. How is the church to see itself in such a world? What is to be its relationship to such a world? What resources can it use to involve itself with such a world?

Getting rid of a false image: The "Christendom" syndrome

Let us first clear the ground by disposing of one view of the relationship of church and world that used to be true and powerful but is now false and powerless. This is a view described by the word Christendom. Although Christianity began as a tiny sect—a handful of Jews in a predominantly Greco-Roman culture—it grew and spread so rapidly that by the fourth century it had become the official religion of the Roman Empire. Increasingly, until the thirteenth century, western culture came under the sway of the church, and religion and culture (ideally at least) were indistinguishable from one another: all life was to be ordered by a Christian commitment and worldview, and all Christians were to submit to God's will, transmitted to them by the church. The cathedral, rather than the courthouse, was to dominate town and city. There was a place for reason, but it was reason crowned by faith, a faith defined by the church. There was room for the state, but it was a state under the moral and even political control of the church; the pope crowned the emperor, not vice versa.

At first glance it would appear that the Reformation demolished all of this, since one of the political by-products of the Reformation was to destroy the overarching unity and divide Europe into smaller countries and rival groups of Christians. Actually, however, the reformers took over the notion of Christendom themselves. They assumed that their own states would be "Christian states," and that within those smaller states there would be one faith, not many: *cuius regio, eius religio* (the religion of the ruler should be the religion of the people). Although kings then refused to bow the knee to popes, the kings (and their court theologians) still insisted that the kings ruled by "divine right." The direct pipeline from God to government was still unchallenged. As a result, Europe became a group of competing "Christendoms," each one claiming that God was on its side, each one eager to conquer or absorb the others. Some of this rubbed off on America's founding fathers, a number of whom desired to plant a "Christian nation" in the wilderness.[11]

The point of this historical excursion is to state as bluntly as possible that *the era of Christendom is over.* Only the willfully blind can pretend that America is a "Christian nation" or even a Protestant nation, that the world embodies a "Christian culture," or that the Church represents a major force in the life of man.

Many churchmen find it exceedingly hard to accept this analysis. They must ponder the fact that whatever the annual increase in church membership it does not keep pace proportionally with an overall population increase and that the number of members taking any active part in church life has decreased. In global terms, "the world" is no longer co-terminus with a "Christian Europe" (if indeed it ever was). The era, then, when we could talk of "Christendom" or a Christian culture or of nations presided over by Christian ideals is past.

Instead of a "Christendom" culture we have a pluralistic culture; instead of a single overarching faith we have many rival and competing faiths; instead of a church personifying the aspirations of all mankind, we have many churches or religious communities, no one of which claims the allegiance of more

[11] Cf., however, the important corrective against pushing this thesis too far on the American scene in F. H. Littell, *From State Church to Pluralism* (New York: Doubleday, 1962).

than a part of mankind. These are the facts, whether church members like them or not, and those who do not like them must come to terms with them, lest they end up inhabiting an unreal, never-never land.[12] A great number of people today have dismissed God from their concerns, and in doing so they profess to feel no great pain.

Affirming the world: New life in old convictions

But the fact that people have dismissed God from their concerns and feel no great pain doing so, does not necessarily mean that God has dismissed people from his concern. For the faith that sustains the church asserts that God continues to concern himself with people and (to carry the parallel even one step further) has done so at great pain. Although proponents of secularism have devalued Christian faith, one of the important claims of the present theological era is that *Christian faith has not devalued proponents of secularism*. For a long time the church's major concern was the church; now it is becoming concerned with the world. For a long time the church was involved with Christians; now it is becoming involved with all humanity. For a long time the church was prepared only to speak; now it is willing to listen. For a long time the church feared scientific advance; now it can embrace it. The end of Christendom, in other words, is not necessarily a tragedy. It can be argued, indeed, that the church is now released from a long introspective chapter of its history and is being turned outward toward the world. It is the *saeculum* rather than the sanctuary that is claiming attention in the sacristy.

Some church members have jumped on the secular bandwagon by disavowing all that came before, wiping their slates clean. This is not a helpful procedure, since it suggests that when the next bandwagon comes along these church members will jump on it with the same uncritical alacrity that has characterized much of the post-Cox "secular city" literature. More useful and more enduring, one hopes, is the attempt to ex-

---

[12] The argument, or course, is not yet complete. It is not enough to dismiss the Christendom image. Some other image (or images) must be put in its place. In subsequent chapters, particularly Chapters 7 and 8, such a discussion will be initiated.

amine the convictions that have been at the center of Christian affirmation and indicate how they can provide a world-affirming stance that thrusts the church onto the frontier of the secular.We will examine four of these, drawing the first two from the insight of Teilhard de Chardin quoted at the beginning of the chapter.

The first of these is a perspective that Christianity shares with Judaism, the doctrine of the world as God's *creation*. In this day and age it is surely not necessary to issue disclaimers about literalistic versions of Genesis in order to insist that a doctrine of creation implies a sense of purposiveness and direction to the world in which the human venture is placed and that we can share in this ongoing creative process. In the light of such a perspective, it is hard to understand how Christians could have developed the kind of aversion to the earthly, temporal, worldly, and secular that some of its proponents have exemplified. The insight that "The earth is the Lord's and the fullness thereof, the world and those who dwell therein" (Psalm 24:1) ought to ensure a high premium being placed on this world and the goods within it. The doctrine of creation, in other words, not only buttresses but necessitates the giving of a positive value to the secular, which is thereby seen as the arena of God's concern and the object of his loving and sustaining power; presumably he would not love and sustain it unless he felt it worth loving and sustaining.

The point is underscored by the further claim that creation is good. The Genesis creation sagas contain the reiterated refrain after each act of creation, "and God saw that it was good," climaxed (after the creation of male and female) by the even more extravagant assessment, "and God saw that it was very good." Here we have the stuff for both positive assessment of the secular arena and a mandate to involve ourselves in it, since God created it, declares his creatures to be his partners in the enterprise of keeping it going, and involves himself in it.[13]

" . . . and involves himself in it. . . ." Here is a second

---

[13] That God chooses "man" to be his partner (symbolized in the Genesis sagas by the command to till the ground and to name the animals) should dispose of the erroneous notion that creation happened once, "back then." Creation must be understood as the ongoing, sustaining activity of God, in which he gives "man" a share and in which we can cooperate in ways that enhance the purposes of creation or rebel in ways that frustrate it.

approach to a theology of the secular, also suggested by the Teilhard insight, the doctrine of the *Incarnation*. The claim is that the very purpose that brought the entire process into being —love—is itself present within that process and is a further step toward the working out of the possibilities inherent in the process. The secular world is not something God shunned, but something with which he has been involved in the most personal kind of involvement possible, namely, in a human life. It is crucial for our understanding of the world that the revelation of God is not centered in mystic withdrawals from the world of matter or timeless truths divorced from history, but squarely in the midst of the rough and tumble of secular history—law courts, politics, battles, food and drink, treachery, storms at sea, soldiers, activities of oppression and liberation, and even, on occasion, organized religion. It is crucial for a Christian understanding of the secular that Jesus lived at a time that can be dated, that he had a "secular" occupation like everybody else, that he spoke Aramaic, that he got hungry, and that his death was ordered by a particular secular ruler, Pontius Pilate.

There have been continuous attempts to "spiritualize" all this and to de-secularize Jesus: Sunday School art has contributed disastrously to the vision of a disembodied spirit wandering around Palestine in a bed sheet. Against all that stands the blunt disavowal of the fourth gospel, "The Word was made flesh and dwelt among us" (John 1:17)—"flesh" being just about the most "un-spiritual" and secular notion that could have occurred to a first-century writer, particularly when he was addressing Greeks who looked upon the world of the flesh as the abode of evil. However, since the Word has been "made flesh," it follows that the world of the flesh has thereby been invested with positive meaning.

Third, the doctrine of *redemption* can be looked on as an important base for a theology of the secular. To "redeem" means to "buy back," to reclaim what was originally one's own; thus redemption is a convenient way of suggesting that even though the world seems to have slipped out of God's control, it has been reclaimed, repossessed, for the purposes of love, and is even now the place where those purposes are being worked out.

Once we begin to think about it, it becomes obvious that the

Bible offers a theology of the world rather than a theology of the church. The best-known verse in the New Testament does not begin "God so loved the Church, that he gave his only begotten Son," but rather "God so loved the world . . ." (John 3:16). The central theme of the New Testament is not "In Christ, God was reconciling the Church unto himself," but rather, "In Christ, God was reconciling the world unto himself" (2 Cor. 5:19). And while selective quotation can produce some slurring New Testament comments about the world, it would be hard to offset the powerful affirmation that "God sent not his Son into the world to condemn the world, but that the world through Him might be saved" (John 3:17). It is interesting that Dietrich Bonhoeffer, starting his theological career with a conviction that Christ is Lord of the church, came at the end to believe that Christ is Lord of the world.[14]

So much would seem clear on a Christian reading of the matter. The object of God's concern is not the church but the world. The church may be a vehicle through which to reach the world, but it is the world that is to be redeemed. However, let us redirect the argument. The New Testament says not only that the world can be redeemed, but that, in the most fundamental sense, it already *is* redeemed: Christ has already subdued the "principalities and powers," he has already won the victory, sin and death have already done their worst to him, and even so the powers of evil have been bested. Surely this is what the imagery of resurrection is communicating. It is the obvious presupposition behind every page of the New Testament.

It is not, of course, at all obvious to twentieth-century readers of the New Testament, particularly if they are members of oppressed minorities to whom any signs of God's victory seem spectacularly lacking. In the face of such lack, we need to remember that the conviction gained credence precisely in the midst of a tiny oppressed minority in the first century, the Jews, who would also have had little reason to believe that this was a correct discerning of "the signs of the times." There is a further analogy drawn from the experience of military combat, where it is likewise seldom obvious what is going on or, more importantly, who is winning. Ian Fraser (drawing on

[14] Cf. the shift in emphasis from D. Bonhoeffer's *The Communion of Saints* (New York: Harper & Row, 1964), first published in 1927 to his *Ethics* (New York: Macmillan, 1955), written 1940–43.

an account by David H. C. Read) tells how on Easter Day, 1945, an advance party of British soldiers captured an allied prisoner of war camp in Germany. And, as Fraser describes it,

> The tables were turned. The captors became captive. Everything faced the other way around. But the advance party had to move on, and there were marauding bands on the loose between the enemy lines. So the ex-prisoners had still to live in their cells. They had to stay behind barbed wire. They had to post sentries. Anyone looking at the camp would have said of them, "These are captives." [But the inmates] knew that effectual deliverance had taken place; that they held the upper hand; that, one day not so far off, deliverance would be rounded out and *all* that it meant would come home to them.[15]

All of this means that God is not only at work in the secular world, but that he is now bringing to completion the victory he has already won in principle. The task of the church, from this view, is to look for those places in the secular arena where God is working out his victory and align itself with what he is doing there. As Luther put it in the imagery of his own day:

> *And though this world with devils filled*
> *Should threaten to undo us,*
> *We will not fear for God has willed*
> *His truth to triumph through us.*

Such a view provides great leverage and insight for church members on the frontier of the secular. In the past, much talk about "the church and the world" has spoken of "taking Christ to . . ." the heathen, the Marxist, or the roommate. But if Christ is *already* lord of the "principalities of powers," then he is in the midst of the world already and was there long before Christians even thought about the matter. Consequently, the church's job is not to take him there, but to find him there, i.e., to discern how and where he is already at work in the world.

Thus, the fourth conviction involves finding God in the

---

[15] I. Fraser, "Nature, World, Principalities" in *Laity, 16,* World Council of Churches (November 1963), p. 12. The point has been made in more formal terms by theologians as diverse as F. D. Maurice, P. T. Forsyth, Edward Schillebeeckx, Karl Barth, and Dietrich Bonhoeffer.

world. But it is not easy to know where to look, particularly since it is implied that we are to look in other than the most obvious or "religious" places. In this connection, it is helpful to think of God as employing pseudonyms, strange names, or even false names (pseudo-names) by means of which to accomplish his purposes and make himself known.[16] Ignazio Silone builds his novel, *Bread and Wine*, around this theme. In it he describes the struggles against fascism in Italy in the 1930's and puts these words in the mouth of Don Benedetto, an elderly priest:

> In times of conspiratorial and secret struggle, the Lord is obliged to hide Himself and assume pseudonyms . . . the Lord does not attach much importance to his name. Might not the ideal of social justice that animates the masses today be one of the pseudonyms the Lord is using to free himself from the control of the churches and the banks? [17]

The "ideal of social justice that animates the masses" in the 1930's in Italy was Italian communism. Don Benedetto is making the surprising statement that the hand of God might be more clearly discerned among Italian communists than among Italian priests or bankers.

This surprising theme, however, is a Biblical theme as well, for there too God is often found where he is least expected. A classic example is the night Jacob spends between Beersheba and Haran. The place he stops at is not a shrine; it has no religious signficance whatever; it is simply where he happened to be when the sun went down. But when he wakes up the next morning after the famous dream in which God appears to him, he says, "Truly the Lord is in this place, and I did not know it" (Genesis 28:16, N.E.B.). That statement and the experience provoking it can stand as a parable for modern Christians as we survey the various movements and activities in the world today. We are called to a new kind of openness

[16] I have developed this theme in considerable detail in *The Pseudonyms of God* (Philadelphia: Westminster Press, 1972), especially Part II; and in "Ignazio Silone and the Pseudonyms of God" in H. J. Mooney and T. F. Staley, eds., *The Shapeless God* (Pittsburgh: University of Pittsburgh Press, 1968).

[17] I. Silone, *Bread and Wine* (New York: Harper & Row, 1946), pp. 247–48.

and a willingness to say with Jacob, "Surely the Lord is in those places and I did not know it." [18]

Such a perspective offers new ways for church members to appraise what is going on in the world around them. It means that God may be doing more about race through the secular civil rights movement than through the Christian churches of America. It means that he may have done more about peace through Buddhist political leaders in Vietnam than through Christian statesmen in America. It means that he may be doing more about brotherhood through the Peace Corps than through a church missionary board. It means that he may be doing more about sensitizing the American conscience through a Jewish rabbi than through a Catholic bishop. Such statements should not be threatening but liberating, suggesting that God is at work in his world in ways that encompass far more than we have dared to believe before.

We must take seriously the suggestion of the French theologian Georges Casalis, which was later incorporated into a number of World Council documents. The traditional way of thinking of God in the world, Casalis says, has been through the sequence, *God-Church-World:* i.e., *God* makes himself known to the *church*, so that the church can take him to the *world*. But, says Casalis, the real sequence should be *God-World-Church:* i.e., *God* is already at work in the *world*, and the *church* is that part of the world that recognizes what he is doing there and tries to align itself and all people with his purposes so that they can be brought to fulfillment.

Symptoms of secular seduction

There are dangers in all of this. Correctives have a habit of becoming norms, and we must indicate four caveats before moving the argument to the next stage:

[18] Other Biblical examples of the unexpectedness of God's appearing are the story of Elijah in the desert, when God does not appear in the usual theophanies of earthquake, wind, and fire, but is unexpectedly present in the still, small voice; the prophecy of Isaiah that in an ensuing battle between Israel and Asyria God will manifest himself in the pagan hosts rather than through his "chosen people"; and the New Testament claim that in a lower-class Jew, son of a carpenter, the supremely unexpected manifestation of God has taken place.

First, there is a danger that an uncritical "theology of the secular" will end up being little more than a repetition of an earlier uncritical "culture-Protestantism," failing to discriminate between those aspects of the secular that are genuine vehicles of God's work and those that may be positively demonic. There is a danger of missing any sense of judgment upon the secular. We may not uncritically affirm all things. Whereas we are to see God at work in the world, we are also to remember that not all that we see in the world is God at work. Father Daniel O'Hanlon, S.J., comments on the problem:

> At one point I have some misgivings. Surely the Christian message is something more than a ratification of the secular, more than a mere discovering of the meaning which already lies hidden in the secular. Has not the redemptive work of Christ given a really new dimension to human history? [19]

Father O'Hanlon is right. Christianity has something to contribute to, as well as draw from, the world of secularity. In affirming the world, the church must not deny what its own heritage can contribute to the world. There is something askew when, as one professor of theology recently complained, "Today everything seems to be a channel of grace except the sacraments." Albert Camus, with his wild cry for meaning in a universe that does not sustain that cry, and his consequent stance of rebellion against the world as it is, may be closer to the fullness of what it means to be a man than the Christian who is ready to bless everything he finds around him.

A second danger is that the uncritical embrace of secularity will lead to the loss of a sense of wonder, of the mystery of human existence, of the dimensions of life that can never adequately be embodied in the freeway or computer. There are what Peter Berger has called "pointers to transcendence"—the laughter, awe, and even judgment that strictly secular analysis cannot account for on its own terms.[20] There is an "over-againstness" of life that the embrace of the secular has difficulty measuring with sufficient seriousness. "Secular man" can easily

---

[19] In W. J. Wolf, ed., *Protestant Churches and Reform Today* (New York: Seabury, 1964), p. 145.

[20] Cf. P. Berger, *A Rumor of Angels* (New York: Doubleday, 1969).

become "flat man," the one whom (for entirely different purposes) Herbert Marcuse describes as "one-dimensional man." The Christian church has "accommodated" too quickly if it is not always living at the edge of wonder.

A third danger is that the Christian will be left historically and institutionally rootless. The thirst for relevance can lead to a denial of what can be learned from experience and history. Many of the creative pioneers on the secular frontier have been institutionally iconoclastic; they do not believe that the church can adopt new roles in a new situation or that the past still has anything to teach them. And while there is need for a healthy iconoclasm (one of the things this book is trying to foster), if the tearing down is not for the sake of building up, the end product is disillusionment or directionlessness of a sort that leads to immobility rather than activity.

The fourth danger is overaffirmation. We need a more dialectical approach to the secular. We must affirm it, but we must not affirm it so uncritically that we can no longer judge it. In espousing "holy worldliness," it is easy to fall into the trap of "compulsive worldliness"—the posture of some church people today whose aim in life seems to be to prove how much more secular they are than their worldly companions. Even in the midst of the affirmation of citizenship in the secular city, Christians must recall that they are still "outsiders" who on occasion have to embody allegiance to a still higher loyalty that may leave their secular commitments doubtful. In an old image into which new life must breathed, Christians are a "pilgrim people," people who live within the *saeculum* but are ever and always on the march, stirred by a divine discontent that gives them no final rest.[21]

Toward greater specificity

We have tried to show that the church must respond affirmatively to the world around it and to suggest that there are resources for doing so within the faith the church proclaims. But it is important to spell this out specifically; in the next two chapters we will examine how this is being done with respect to the frontier of revolution and the frontier of technology.

[21] For the development of this and other images see Chapters 7 and 8.

4

The Frontier of Revolution

The question is not whether revolution will come,
but whether it will come violently or nonviolently.
—Thomas Melville, former
Maryknoll priest in Guatemala

Those who make peaceful revolution impossible will
make violent revolution inevitable.
—John F. Kennedy

A watershed in church thinking about contemporary frontiers occurred in July 1966 when the World Council of Churches sponsored a conference at Geneva on "Christians in the Technical and Social Revolutions of Our Time." This conference marked the first time that a world conference of Christians had had a majority of lay rather than clerical voices, the "third world" (i.e., South America, India, Asia, and Africa) had had significant representation and a powerful voice, and the reality of a world in revolution had been directly confronted by church leaders.[1]

As the conference title indicates, two "revolutions" were examined. The first of these was the social or political revolution, stemming from the inequities between the rich and the poor nations (as well as inequities within them) and the need to find ways of redressing the grotesquely unjust imbalances that result. The second revolution was the technological revolution, brought about by the highly refined electronic techniques

[1] Cf. P. Abrecht and M. M. Thomas, eds., *World Conference on Church and Society* (Geneva: W.C.C., 1971). The term "third world" comes from a conference of so-called "uncommitted" nations meeting at Bandung in 1955, seeking for a way other than that represented by the "worlds" of capitalism and communism. As a term it is too all-inclusive, but it does provide a shorthand pointer to the two-thirds of the human family that is poor and colored.

of automation and cybernation that make it possible to control the many aspects of our environment.

The two revolutions are interrelated, since advanced technology enhances and actually increases a nation's economic superiority, but it will be useful to separate them for purposes of discussion. The present chapter deals with the reality of political and social revolution, and the following chapter with the technological revolution.

Facts that underline the revolutionary situation today

For a number of years ecumenical discussion was dominated by the theme of "rapid social change," with particular reference to Asia, Africa, India, and Latin America. It now appears that "rapid social change" is a euphemism for "revolution." It is beyond doubt that major sections of the world are in the midst of "revolution," in the sense that radical social change is either being sought or is actually taking place, that it is taking place rapidly, and that if it does not take place rapidly enough by nonviolent means it will take place by violent means. To understand why this is so, we need do little more than examine a few salient facts about the world today, and anyone who can relate to Bishop Gore's definition of love as "the ability to read statistics with compassion" will be hard put to avoid some uncomfortable conclusions:

- At the present time about 20 per cent of the people of the world control 80 per cent of the world's resources.
- An average of 15,000 people starve to death each day.
- Every night two-thirds of the world's peoples go to bed hungry, if they even have a bed to which to go.
- Half the people of the world have a per capita income of under $100 a year.
- In 1970 the *increase* in the gross national product of the United States was equal to the *entire* gross national product of the continent of Africa. Americans had more for luxuries than Africans had for everything.

A geographical and racial breakdown of the world's resources makes clear that the areas of greatest economic wealth are located in the northern hemisphere, whereas the areas of greatest economic poverty are located in the southern hemisphere—a situation exacerbated by the fact that this distribution corresponds generally to the respective location of the white and colored peoples of the world. Whether one examines the world in terms of such issues as per capita gross national product, infant mortality rate, the per capita number of physicians and dentists, or the incidence of malnutrition, with almost no significant exceptions the breakdown follows a similar pattern: the white nations of the north are extraordinarily rich, the colored nations of the south are extraordinarily poor.

By 1960 these facts were already alarming enough so that the United Nations instituted a "Decade of Development," in which the "developed" nations were urged to make special efforts, through loans and gifts of money and resources, to begin to close this gap so that the "underdeveloped" nations might enter into markets for world trade and bring their standard of living closer to the necessities for a minimally decent life. But at the end of the first Decade of Development, the disparities between rich and poor were proportionately greater than they had been at the beginning of the decade. Conclusion: we live in a world in which, in relation to one another, the rich are getting richer while the poor are getting poorer.[2]

This is the stuff from which revolutions are made. There is no reason to believe that in a world in which the rich are getting richer and the poor are getting poorer, the poor will continue indefinitely to accept these ugly conditions, particularly when the poor comprise a great majority of the human family and the rich a relatively small minority. When we add the racial component that by and large the rich are white and the poor are colored, the historical component that the rich white minority has systematically exploited the poor colored majority in the past, and the psychological component that the poor now know that this is the case and that there is no reason for it to remain the case—then we have a situation that is explosive.

[2] For an elaboration of the material in the above paragraph, cf. *inter alia,* M. D. Bryant, *A World Broken by Unshared Bread* (Geneva: W.C.C., 1970); R. Dickinson, *Line and Plummet* (Geneva: W.C.C., 1968); *In Search of a Theology of Development* (Geneva: SODEPAX, 1970).

Meeting economic injustice by supplying economic aid

What should the churches be doing about this situation? The question should particularly concern the "established" churches, since they have been the beneficiaries of the economies of the rich white nations that have been guilty of exploiting the poor colored nations. To the degree that white churches have acquiesced in exploitation, they have a particular responsibility to reverse it. Taking for granted that it is the job of the church to minister to the whole person and not just a disembodied soul, much ecumenical church support has been given to projects designed to give economic aid to underdeveloped nations.[3]

Using the professional expertise drawn from the fields of banking, economics, political science, and world economic development, the World Council of Churches and the Pontifical Commission on Justice and Peace have joined forces in backing proposals to provide resources, through an international monetary pool, so that developing nations can acquire capital to improve their own economies and thus enter world trade markets without being at such an overwhelming disadvantage. Recognizing that expert advice is needed to deal with specific decisions about interest rates, long-term vs. short-term loans compared to outright gifts, and the relationship of monetary aid to goods and manpower services, the ecumenical agencies have provided criteria or guidelines for those making such decisions. The joint Vatican and World Council Commission on Society, Development, and Peace (SODEPAX) noted the failure of the first United Nations "Decade of Development" and suggested the following overall principle to guide an approach to the next decade:

> Compassion and justice demand that we start from a perception of what social objectives are minimally acceptable for a life that is consistent with the Christian con-

[3] Details of such proposals can be found in the official reports of the 1966 Geneva Conference cited above; the Beiruit Conference of 1968, and the report of the fourth-world assembly of the World Council of Churches at Uppsala, in 1968; all available from the World Council of Churches in Geneva.

cept of man created in the image of God. We then work outwards and backwards from that perception to discover what changes must be made in the policies of both the rich nations and the poor to assure that all men are given access to that quality of life within the foreseeable future.[4]

This is not quite as innocuous as it sounds. It means that the starting point is not the imbalance of the *status quo*, nor is it an assumption that the life of people in India should resemble that of people in Indiana. The norms of Anglo-Saxon culture are not to be imposed upon other cultures. Some points that can be derived from this overall principle follow:

1. The achievement of the stated objective "would require substantial changes in the power structure of the world." A power structure that works to the advantage of the rich and the disadvantage of the poor will never permit a redress of the imbalances. This is threatening to those with power, since it implies that no peripheral tinkering with present economic structures will produce the degree of change needed.

2. Even the meeting of minimal social objectives will involve "a drastic reduction in sums presently spent on arms throughout the world." The fact that the United States alone spends two-thirds of its national budget on arms is some indication of how drastically unbalanced the use of national resources has become. To divert even a small fraction of the military budget to economic and social rehabilitation would make an inestimable difference to mankind. Yet the likelihood of persuading the American people to take such a "risk" is slight.

3. Economic aid can no longer be given unilaterally, and SODEPAX has recognized "the inadequacy of the nation-state as a means to full development." Economic aid must go through international agencies if it is to avoid being a new and subtle form of "economic colonialism."

4. Decisions about economic aid can no longer be made only or even chiefly by the givers of aid but must be made in constant discussion with those who are to be the recipients of aid. The recipients must determine the direction of their own economic development.

[4] *Partnership or Privilege* (Geneva: SODEPAX, 1971), pp. 10–11.

The churches should introduce these points into any discussion of economic aid. In addition, there are certain further considerations that can be addressed particularly to the churches themselves.[5]

1. The churches must insist that the human dimension is central in the consideration of social objectives. Otherwise decisions are often economic and political.

2. Because churches have an international network, they have a special responsibility to inform their constituencies and all decision-making bodies throughout the world of the realities of the present situation. This can be done by analyzing the economy, by calling attention to the realities of present oppressive political structures, and by providing a voice and a world forum through which the anguish of the oppressed can be heard.

3. Within the rich nations, the churches have an obligation to use whatever political leverage they have to sensitize the consciences of the rich and the powerful to the need for change. Although Christians are a minority without much power, they still represent the kind of minority that, if mobilized, could be the "swing-vote" in bringing about legislation for economic aid.

4. Since the churches have investments of their own, they must set an example by re-examining their own investment portfolios. Many of them support institutions that foster racial injustice or economic imperialism, and they can hardly recommend enlightened aid on an international level if such financial support is continued.

5. The church has a particular pastoral responsibility to prepare its own members for the fact that radical change must come and that such change will inevitably work some pain and hardship on all those above the poverty level. Espousal of almost any of the points cited above will bring the church into conflict with many of the most powerful segments of society and will alienate much of its own constituency as well. Realistically the choice will not finally be whether to engage in conflict or not, but in which conflict to become engaged. The

[5] For an elaboration of these and the following points, cf. *ibid*, pp. 11–13.

church can engage in conflict with those segments of its own culture resisting change, or, by walking fearfully away from that conflict, it can hasten the arrival of a much wider and more fundamental conflict—a worldwide conflict between those who have much more than their share and those who have been systematically denied all but the barest minimum necessary for survival.

The critique of proposals for economic aid

One might assume that the approach described above would gain the cautious support of concerned citizens in rich nations and the eager support of those in poor nations, since it is an attempt to alleviate the economic injustices that are an affront to the human conscience. This is far from the case, however, and there has been a significant critique of the approach, coming in large part from the would-be recipients of such economic aid. Some of the reasons for disenchantment are listed here.[6]

1. Economic aid does not get to the root of the problem, which is the injustice of the entire economic order. It is argued that the present proposals skirt a system that is fundamentally unjust and that all that will ever happen is that a little goods and money will trickle down from the very rich to the very poor; the very rich will not be seriously inconvenienced, and the very poor will never get enough to become more than passive recipients of aid that will not significantly relieve their plight. The present imbalances will thus be perpetuated indefinitely, with only enough token help given to keep the poor from rising up in outraged rebellion.

2. These proposals for economic aid perpetuate a paternalistic relationship between donor and recipient. The poor remain dependent upon the rich. Although nineteenth-century political colonialism has now in principle been transcended by the political independence of developing nations, it has in fact

---

[6] Cf. further on these themes A. van Leeuwen, *Development through Revolution* (New York: Scribners, 1970); R. Laurentin, *Liberation, Development and Salvation* (Maryknoll: Orbis Books, 1972); and G. Gutierrez, *A Theology of Liberation* (Maryknoll: Orbis Books, 1972).

been replaced by an economic colonialism. Even when the economic controls are subtle, the human controls are inexorable. A particularly clear example of this is offered by Ivan Illich, who notes that many Americans have been eager to provide hospitals for Mexico. But Illich points out that hospitals are a luxury available only to well-to-do, upper-class citizens. The introduction of large hospitals in Mexico would benefit only wealthy segments of the Mexican population. What Mexico really needs instead of hospitals, he insists, is thousands of small-town clinics, and instead of skilled surgeons it needs thousands of midwives who can assist in childbirth in out-of-the-way places. And this is only one example of the way donors seek to impose their standards on the recipients of their *largesse*.

3. The poor nations look with suspicion on the motivations for economic aid offered by the rich nations, since they do not believe that rich nations would support programs that would jeopardize their economic superiority. Aid that would make a difference might threaten many if not most of the markets the rich nations now control. So representatives of the poor nations see economic aid as no more than a palliative designed to keep the poor in submission.

4. Countries that receive the most aid tend to have repressive and totalitarian governments. It is these regimes rather than progressive or left-wing forces that receive aid, since the rich nations feel that they are "bulwarks against communism," able to put down, by the economic and military aid provided by rich nations, any uprisings or revolutions that might threaten the economic investments of the rich nation in the poor country or the ideology of the rich nation. Economic aid given under such circumstances tends to shore up repressive regimes and to make it even more difficult than before to see that minimal justice is available to all within the country.

The real problem is not the abuse of power by the majority of people in the world today, since they do not have any power to abuse; it is the abuse of power by the generally white minority that controls most of the world markets and many of the political structures and that has the military power to enforce its will or whim. It is clear that the exploited peoples of the world are increasingly unwilling to accept their exploitation passively and that, if radical change is not brought about in peaceful ways (significant relinquishments of power on the part of the white minority), change will be brought about in violent ways (increasing determination of the exploited majority to achieve self-determination by whatever means are necessary, whether nonviolent or violent). Thus, no examination of the frontier of revolution is complete until there has been some discussion of violence.[7]

The problem of violence

Let us begin with two assumptions derived from the previous discussion.

The first assumption is that the problem of violence or nonviolence is subordinate to the problem of power: Will we use power responsibly or irresponsibly, creatively or destructively? It is particularly important for Americans to remember how central the issue of power really is, since Americans have the most power and have proved to be particularly adept at abusing it. That power can be exercised by the use of violence is self-evident. That power might also be exercised by the use of nonviolence deserves attention.

The second assumption is that we have limited the definition of violence to overt physical destruction against persons or institutions. We have failed to realize that there is also covert or hidden violence built into the very structure of our society. This can be described as the violence of the *status quo* in which societal structures are so rigged in the favor of a privileged class that certain groups lack the opportunity to better themselves; or it can be described as institutional violence, represented by zoning laws that condemn certain groups to inferior housing or poor education.

One of the most astute theologians of the "third world,"

[7] What follows is no more than an introduction to issues raised by "the problem of violence." I have pursued this theme in considerably greater detail in *Religion and Violence* (Philadelphia: Westminster Press, 1973), giving special attention to the input of thinking from "third-world" Christians, and some of that material has been used in these pages.

Professor José Miguez-Bonino of Brazil, sums up these assumptions:

> An ethic of revolution cannot avoid discussing the question of the use and justification of violence. This question, nevertheless, needs to be placed in its proper perspective as a subordinate and relative question. It is subordinate because it has to do with the "cost" of the desired change —the question of the legitimacy of violence and vice versa. "Violence" is a cost that must be estimated and pondered in relation to a particular revolutionary situation. It is relative because in most revolutionary situations —at least in those with which we are concerned [in South America]—violence is already a fact constitutive of the situation—injustive, slave labor, hunger, and exploitation are forms of violence that must be weighed against the cost of revolutionary violence.[8]

We live in a world of covert violence, so that fundamental change is mandatory, and change will come through the constructive (or destructive) use of power. These realities force us to pose the question: In rooting out the structures of covert violence in the world today, are we justified in using overt violence? The Christian must accept the fact that the direction and nature of society need changing. The question then becomes one of means: Is the change to come by violent or nonviolent means? The answer is not easy, for those who simplistically opt for violence must be reminded that they may be jeopardizing the vision of peace, whereas those who simplistically opt for nonviolence must be reminded that they may be ignoring the cry for justice wrung from the heart of the oppressed.

Most of Christian history is a sorry history of justifying the Christian use of overt physical violence in the name of whatever the justifier was trying to defend at the moment. However, there is this difference in the current discussion: whereas historically Christians have tended to justify violence as an instrument of the oppressor, many who advocate its use today insist that it may be used only on behalf of the oppressed. Such a distinction can be simplistic; but, it cannot be simply

---

[8] J. Miguez-Bonino, *Development Apocalypse* (Geneva: W.C.C., 1967), p. 108.

dismissed. As the German theologian Jürgen Moltmann has pointed out, "Those who advocate nonviolence today are usually those who control police power. Those who embrace violence are usually those who have no means of power." [9]

The case today for overt violence grows out of a belief that covert violence is so deep-seated, and so powerfully entrenched, that only overt violence can remove from power those who practice covert violence. It is indeed intolerable that 20 per cent of the world's people should control 80 per cent of the world's wealth or that in a given country a military dictatorship representing 5 per cent of the people should control the destinies of the other 95 per cent. Covert violence is so bad, the argument runs, that overt violence to overthrow it is not only permissible but is demanded in the name of social justice, equality, and love. To shrink from overt violence on a relatively small scale means supporting or at least condoning covert violence on a large scale.

The failure to examine this position seriously betrays a mind that is closed to the contemporary world. Helmut Gollwitzer, a German theologian, recently commented on this perplexing fact, out of his experience that the brutality of war was leading to a new articulation of pacifism in Europe. And yet,

> Just at this moment when we . . . are inclined to regard as mistaken the traditional approval of Christian participation in the use of military force and to hoist the flag of pacifism . . . we hear from our brethren in the under-developed countries (where the situation is a revolutionary one) that they consider it incumbent upon them to participate in the national and social revolutionary struggles which involve the use of force.[10]

What kinds of problems are involved if this position is adopted?

There is a danger in extrapolating too quickly from a third-world situation of a military or an economic dictatorship to another situation and insisting that the two cases are parallel,

---

[9] J. Moltmann, *Religion, Revolution and the Future* (New York: Scribners, 1969).

[10] Cited in M. E. Marty and D. G. Peerman, eds., *New Theology, No. 6* (New York: Macmillan, 1969), p. 113.

so that what is appropriate in one case is appropriate in the other. The degree of seriousness with which one argues for violent revolution in the United States will depend upon the degree to which one does or does not believe there are still other options for change available in the United States. Whites must be sensitive at this point: if we say we believe there are other options short of violence we must be sure that we are not merely exhibiting comfortable, white, middle-class reflexes. Blacks and members of other minority groups may long since have come to feel that all other alternatives have been exhausted.

A question that can be raised about the Christian espousal of violence is: Are we willing to pay the price? One might believe that in some parts of the world a violent *coup* might really strike a blow for justice and still be staggered by the romantic unrealism of those who feel that a similar movement in the United States could succeed. There is no doubt what would happen; as Governor Reagan of California, with the National Guard at his disposal, said of university students, "If they want a bloodbath, let's give them one right now."

Another question is to be pondered: How does violence affect not only those who are its victims but also those who employ it? There is an extraordinarily slippery slope from the violence-against-property-but-not-against-people theme to the violence-against-people-here-is-okay-because-there-is-more-violence-against-people-somewhere-else point of view. There is almost always more violence somewhere else, and the ugly grip violence gets on people can increasingly undermine the most idealistic ends to which it is being dedicated. Before long, all restraints are gone. The theme of so many of Ignazio Silone's novels—that when the persecuted seize power they always become persecutors—is a theme we must never underplay.

Considerations such as these are part of the case made by those who opt for nonviolence as the proper Christian stance.

Some Christians adopt the position of absolute pacifism, insisting that there are no circumstances in which overt violence is justified. This position has the advantage of being rooted in the New Testament and the early church—so that the initial burden is always on the Christian who rejects it rather than on the Christian who affirms it. As the special witness of a minority, it has exerted a creative restraint on other, less single-minded individuals and institutions far out of proportion to the numbers of its adherents. The problem is that however effective it may be in the long run, the pacifist stance may temporarily enhance injustice. Christians must be concerned about the short-run consequences of their actions, particularly when those actions determine the justice or injustice available to others.

Other Christians argue that violence can be used only as a last resort, when all other options have failed. One must, therefore, develop criteria to determine when violence might or might not be appropriate. This process resembles the traditional approach of Roman Catholic theology to develop criteria for determining a "just war."

It is useful to take those criteria and apply them not just to international war but to the entire matter of violence. They would seem to lead one to become a "selective conscientious objector" to most uses of violence. Let us look at two examples. One principle is that the employment of violence must have a good chance of success, i.e., it must clearly lead to greater social justice and not to indiscriminate slaughter or repression. Another principle, the "principle of proportionality," states that the means used must be in harmony with the ends sought, and the good end hoped for must be assured of producing greater benefits than the evils that will be entailed along the way toward that good end by the use of violence.

A white American may not be entitled to tell minority Americans, or oppressed Brazilians, what their stance on violence should be, since he is neither a minority nor oppressed, though he may point out that César Chavez has made nonviolence the key to the whole struggle of Mexican-Americans for social justice and that Archbishop Helder Camara, a revolutionary if there ever was one, has insisted that a new order in Brazil can come only by nonviolent means. Both make clear that nonviolence need not be the moral copout of the middle class.

A white American may, however, be entitled to suggest that the vocation of nonviolent militancy is an appropriate vocation for white, middle-class, comfortable Americans. In a world and in a nation more and more accustomed to violence as the easy answer to all problems, it may be a special vocation to take on the role of nonviolent advocates of social change. It would mean looking for new ways and means to incarnate a love that is not devoid of the most passionate concern for justice; it would mean attacking the structures of injustice and covert violence in the social system, but not in ways that would transform the attackers into the kind of people and structures they are trying to replace; it would mean an attempt to deal creatively with tension, rather than escaping from it. It would entail certain risks. Martin Luther King told blacks in the sixties to be nonviolent against angry white mobs. If he were alive in the seventies, might he be telling whites to be nonviolent against angry black mobs?

Is there a special role for the church?

It may be that the questions and suggestions of the previous paragraph are unrealistic for white, middle-class Americans. But are they also unrealistic for white, middle-class, American Christians?

Is it possible for the church to play a unique role in the events of the next decades in which the struggle for peace must be joined with the struggle for justice? From all that has been said, it should be clear that it is basically the task of the church to be for creative change for the dispossessed, rather than (as has so often been true in its history) for the *status quo* and thereby against the dispossessed. Thus, the church must be on the side of revolution, understood as the attempt to bring about rapid social change, and the American church may have a special calling to be on the side of *nonviolent* revolution. There is no assurance that this will "work" in the sense that the fact that some white Christians are committed to nonviolence will make nonviolence a powerful instrument for social change, though there is always the outside possibility that it will. Short of such a consequence there is still an increasing need for the kind of minority witness that might persuade others to think again about the violent structures, both overt and covert, that have come to characterize America's domestic life and foreign policy under a number of presidents.

Professor James Cone, a black theologian, has said that in this day and age blacks are not called upon to suffer but to be free, and that in the past white Christians were quite willing to let black Christians embrace the vocation of suffering. He points out that "black theology" must work out ways to achieve the liberation of blacks from the bondage imposed upon them by whites. There are some disturbing implications in this analysis for white Christians as well. In an era when the black vocation is not to suffer but to be free, it may be that the white vocation is the willingness to risk suffering and put a certain amount of white "freedom" on the line, taking the considerable risk that out of this a new liberation can come for both blacks and whites. While the Christian gospel does not urge people to seek suffering, it does remind Christians that they may be called upon to risk suffering on behalf of new possibilities for others.

Consequently, in defining a special role for the white Christian churches in the 1970's, it should be understood that in addition to the political pressures church people are called upon to exercise in working toward greater social justice, they are also called upon to seek a role that will bring about change by nonviolent means, the role of revolutionary love, with a willingness to absorb the suffering this might involve. The minute such a role leads to a moral copout, enabling Christians to escape conflict, it must be vigorously repudiated. It must be clear that revolutionary love is not a means of avoiding conflict but rather a means of dealing with it, if such love is to have any effect on the American scene.

Let us carry the argument a step further. Christians must be aware that any decision to opt for social change, whether violent or nonviolent, will turn the church into what Professor Fals Borda, a Colombian sociologist, has described as a "subverting" community. Rather than shoring up present economic, political, and social systems that perpetuate economic, political, and social injustice, Professor Borda insists that the church must actively try to undermine such parts of the system as are not conducive to growth for all peoples. He insists that Jesus Christ was a "subversive" in terms of the society in which he lived and that at its best the church has sought a similar role. Only when it denied its vocation to subvert whatever was wrong in the society around it did the church become the captive of that society. Jan Hus, John Wycliffe, Martin Luther,

John Calvin, George Fox, and all the other great "reformers" of the church can only be understood as subversive of both the ecclesiastical and social structures of their times. "When the wheel of history comes back upon itself," Professor Borda comments, "it is recognized that the ones who were really against society were rather those who defended an unjust social order held to be just simply because it was traditional." [11]

What all this means for the church's future has been indicated by Paul Abrecht, Executive Secretary of the Department of Church and Society of the World Council of Churches.[12] He notes that churches in the west must learn to live with the knowledge that the center of history is moving away from them, not only in terms of ecclesiastical influence but of political influence as well. The future will not be in Europe or North America, but in Asia, Africa, and Latin America. Thus, the most extensive American participation in the ecumenical movement is necessary to liberate the American church from parochialism. It means that American Christians must first of all listen to African, Asian, and Latin American Christians and make their own decisions in the light of what they hear. It means that such newly acquired ecumenical insight must be brought to bear on the way American churches deal with American domestic and foreign policy and that ways must be found to exert pressure on the instruments of American foreign policy that are instruments of covert and overt aggression and violence against smaller nations. It means that the American church must search for ways in which it can show greater solidarity with the churches of Asia, Africa, and Latin America, who must of necessity support forces in their own countries working for revolutionary change. Without the perspective made possible by this measure of engagement on the ecumenical scene, it is hard to see how American Christians can deal creatively with the frontier of revolution. Apart from such perspective, there will be an inevitable temptation to lapse into parochial and uncritical ways of viewing the

[11] *IDOC*, International North American edition (Oct. 17, 1970), New York, p. 47.
[12] P. Abrecht, "The Revolution Implicit in Development," *Christianity and Crisis* (June 23, 1969), pp. 178–81.

actions of the United States on the world scene, and such parochial and uncritical attitudes can only hasten the time when, as John F. Kennedy predicted, those who have made peaceful revolution impossible will have made violent revolution inevitable.

The miracle that is called for

The prescription is a demanding and in some ways bitter prescription that has no sugar-coating; it prescribes that those with power relinquish at least some of that power voluntarily. There is little historical precedent to suggest that the demand will be met. And yet if it is not, the consequences will be appalling. The American church, as an institution of one of the most powerful nations on earth, clearly has a role to play, a role that it will embrace to the degree that it remembers that it is part of a worldwide fellowship with loyalties much more encompassing than mere national loyalties.

Under the very best of circumstances, what is called for is on the order of a miracle, and Archbishop Helder Camara has most succinctly described what will constitute that miracle. What Dom Helder calls for is a people and a church who will be "fit instruments to perform the miracle of combining the violence of the prophets, the truth of Christ, the revolutionary spirit of the gospel—but without destroying love." [13]

[13] H. Camara, *Church and Colonialism* (London: Sheed and Ward, 1969), p. 111.

5

The Frontier of Technology

Adam (to Eve as they are being driven out of the Garden of Eden by a cherubim with a flaming sword): "My dear, we live in an age of transition."
                                                —*New Yorker* cartoon

We have seen that the political and technological revolutions are not separable save for the temporary purpose of systematic discussion. As we move to the frontier of technology it is important to remind ourselves of the interrelationship, for the social and technological revolutions are not only co-existent in time, but co-determinative in effect. Thus, those nations with technological expertise today have a tremendous advantage in terms of political power; those nations lacking such expertise are at an extraordinary disadvantage, their ability to engage in trade to their own economic advantage being hampered by their lack of technology. We have already seen that the distance between developed and developing nations is increasing rather than decreasing, and it becomes increasingly clear to third-world nations that their economic well-being will come not by trickle-down help through "economic development" but by the liberation that comes through the political overthrow of unjust internal regimes and political disengagement from the ideologies of the rich nations. But the problem of gaining technological expertise in order to compete for world markets still remains.

Furthermore, as technological power increases, it takes fewer people to manage it, but these technologists require a higher degree of training. Thus even though the population of America may decrease proportionately in relation to the rest of the earth, the technological superiority America now has means that fewer people have the potential to control more people.

The ambiguity of technological advance

One of the most perplexing problems in trying to assess technological advance is that a bewildering variety of interpretations can be put upon the same data. There is not even agreement about the appropriate terminology. Daniel Bell talks about a "post-industrial society," in which technology is capable of self-sustaining growth. Kenneth Boulding speaks of "post-civilization," to contrast the volatile future society with the era of settled communities, e.g., the "civilization" we now know. Zbigniew Brzezinski speaks of the "technotronic society," one based on advanced communications and electronics; Marshall McLuhan describes an electronic age of communications in which mankind inhabits a "global village"; Alvin Toffler speaks of a "super-industrial" society, meaning "a complex, fast-paced society, dependent upon extremely advanced technology and a post-materialist value system." [1]

Even more puzzling is the ambiguity with which the experts assess the technological era. To some it is clearly a blessing, helping humankind escape from an era of darkness and superstition, and there are almost no limits to the creative use people can make of the tools now at their disposal. R. Buckminster Fuller is one of the clearest prophets of the liberation the new age promises. Such writers stress our control of technology.

There are also those who see such advance as a curse. To them the liabilities far outweigh the gains, for we are becoming enslaved; indeed they feel that we may already be so enslaved by technique that it is too late to reverse the process. The clearest prophet of enslavement is Jacques Ellul, who feels that it is virtually impossible for us to move in ways that could release us from the box which has trapped us. Such writers stress technology's control over us.

Some see both the problems and the perils and stress the need for a high degree of control or planning to ensure Utopia rather than Armageddon, sometimes without defining what the criteria for control should be or who should control the controllers of the controlling process. Both admirers and critics of B. F. Skinner might place him in this position.[2] Another

---

[1] On the above cf. A. Toffler, *Future Shock* (New York: Random House, 1970), Chapter I and pp. 443–34.
[2] Cf. on this whole problem, J. H. Burke, ed. *The New Technology and Human Values* (Belmont, Calif.: Wadsworth, 1966).

way to state this third viewpoint is to dismiss as simplistic the contrast stated above between "our control of technology" and "technology's control over us," and to describe the situation in terms of a dynamic *interface*. This widely used term has been elaborated by William Kuhns to mean "the process initiated between two systems." A simple example of interface is a bicycle rider, who must learn to "monitor feedback and adjust." To some degree the bicycle controls the rider, but to some degree also the rider controls the bicycle.[3]

Two further problems

Such ambiguities pose two further unresolved problems that must engage the attention of the church on the technological frontier. One of these centers on whether the technological era represents a qualitatively new situation or whether it is just a contemporary re-statement of a continuing situation. It is tempting (and theologically comforting) to believe that every new problem is only a re-statement of an old problem and, since we always live "in an age of transition," that it is foolish to panic in the face of what now seems a mysterious unknown. According to this view, we are merely confronting the old problems in new forms: Are we free? What is good? How do we decide?

On the other hand, it can be argued that there are brand-new problems we have not had to face before. The old problem was how to control nature, but the development of technological expertise could now solve much of that problem. Thanks to astrodomes we do not call off ball games because of rain, and thanks to floodlights we do not call them off because of darkness. We can now, if we wish to pay the price, transport water so that the desert can blossom as the rose, and we can make rain when the right kinds of clouds are there to seed. The job is not how to control "nature" but how to control "society" so that our control of nature will not exploit it for the benefit of the few in ways that lead to our common downfall.

The *rate of change* in the technological era is so quantita-

[3] Cf. W. Kuhns, *Environmental Man* (New York: Harper & Row, 1969).

tively rapid that the total effect may be qualitatively new. In his dizzying report, *Future Shock*, Alvin Toffler is serious in asking whether we will be able to keep pace with the rapidity of change. The computer does quickly what the human brain takes much longer to do, but does it with such incredible rapidity that one can argue that it does indeed create a "new" situation. Robert Theobald suggests that there are four fundamental drives arising from the application of computer systems that create totally new dynamic forces. These are: "the drive toward unlimited destructive power, the drive toward unlimited productive power, the drive to eliminate the human mind from repetitive activities, and the inherent organizational drive of computer systems." [4] As U Thant puts it, describing the second of these truths, "It is no longer resources that limit decisions. It is the decision that makes the resources . . . . This is the fundamental revolutionary change—perhaps the most revolutionary mankind has ever known." [5]

The question, "Can we do this? used to mean, "Do the rules allow it?" A manager could not change the distance from home plate to the left-field fence during the ball game and had to decide whether to walk Hank Aaron or pitch to him on the basis of that given fact. But today, the question "Can we do this?" no longer means, "Do the rules allow it?" but rather, "Can we change the rules?" or even "We can change the rules." It is now possible for the first time, as Emmanuel Mesthene puts it, to move the left-field fence during the game.[6] We now have enough expertise to change the rules as we go along: medical researchers can change some of the rules about when individuals die; government and industry can change some of the rules about how long the planet earth will be habitable; transportation agencies can change some of the rules about getting from Spitzbergen to Nome by offering a water route under the polar icecap; electronic experts can change some of the rules about modes of communication so that *how* we communicate determines *what* we communicate.

A second set of problems centers around whether or not

[4] In D. Munby, ed., *Economic Growth in World Perspective* (New York: Association Press, 1966), p. 158.

[5] *Ibid*, p. 159.

[6] Cf. C. E. Silberman and *Fortune* Magazine Editors, *The Myths of Automation* (New York: Harper & Row, 1966), pp. 113–14.

technology is neutral. Many argue that technology is around for good or for ill and that it is solely up to us to decide what is done with it. A graphic case can be made for placing us at the crossroads of decision, on the brink of producing an earthly heaven or hell—two roads diverge in our yellow wood and we can walk down either one. The problem remains a human problem.

But here the somber note introduced by Ellul becomes important: we could still choose the road less traveled by and it might make all the difference, except that it may be too late, or it may be that the options are unfairly weighted; technique may already be controlling us, persistently eroding our freedom and subverting our values. The sorcerer's apprentice can no longer count on the sorcerer to return with a cease and desist formula. If this is so, technique is not neutral; it is poised on the side of dehumanization, despite what Fuller, McLuhan, and others say about its ability to lift us out of old limitations into new possibilities.

A further refinement of the argument is contained in the realization that much technological "advancement" is self-generated, i.e., it takes place for its own sake. The ability to build a bigger computer because of the expertise developed from the use of little computers means almost inevitably that the bigger computer will be built. If more sophisticated weaponry is possible then we had better have it. Our ability to detonate a hydrogen bomb one mile under the Aleutian Islands had an irresistible attraction to the policy-makers even though the consequences if something went wrong would have been appalling. Technological expertise has inverted Kant's maxim so that it no longer reads, "I ought, therefore I can," but rather, "I can, therefore I ought," and even, "I can, therefore I must."

One example, however, suggests that the trend is not yet irreversible. This is the fact that although we are technologically able to design and construct bigger and faster airplanes, we are not inevitably committed to doing so. Further input into all the problems involved, such as ecological considerations, can still bring people to the point where they can say "no" to building something simply because it can be built. A far-reaching turning point in the tendency of technology to "take over" may have been attained when the United States

Senate voted to terminate construction of the supersonic transport. *Homo faber* has not yet become *homo fabricatus;* the architect has not yet become the artifact. But even this victory is fragile; pressures are constantly exerted to renew the project.

The impact of technology on human beings

But there is still a possibility that the architect will become the artifact, that the person who used to make things will "be made" by things, that creativity will be stifled, choices circumscribed, potentiality for the future chipped away so that we become the prisoner of our very ingenuity. Herbert Marcuse argues with great forcefulness that "one-dimensional man" is the end product of the technological era and that we have been so programmed by our culture that critical thinking and action are no longer possible. Rubem Alves underlines the point:

> Technology creates a false man, a man who learns how to find happiness in what is given to him by the system. His soul is created as the image of what he can have. To the extent to which the system creates new needs and provides the objects to satisfy these needs, it is able to keep man an integral part of itself . . . . The success of the system in the delivery of goods now provides the basis for the ideological justification and practical self-perpetuation. Whatever delivers goods must be true.[7]

The very mention of Alves, a third-world theologian, reminds us of the sense in which a "class" consciousness operates to determine many of our attitudes. Those who are most upset by the "corrupting influence of technology," turn out to be those from affluent cultures who have more of everything (thanks to technology) than they can possibly need or use. White, middle-class panygyrics against technology sound increasingly hollow and hypocritical to people from underdeveloped areas of the world. Two-thirds of the human family has never had a chance to be corrupted by an overabundance of goods, and they properly resent being told by the white minority of that family that the introduction of technology

---

[7] R. Alves, *A Theology of Human Hope* (Washington: Corpus Books, 1969), p. 23.

can bring spiritual ruin in its wake. (At the Amsterdam assembly of the World Council of Churches in 1948, European and American delegates were preparing a condemnation of technology for having contributed to the spiritual emptiness of modern life. Bishop Rajah Manikam of India commented, "Before you condemn technology, will you let us have it, please, in India for fifty years?") Granted that the sudden advent of technology in the life of a primitive culture may induce culture shock of the first order, many of the initial fruits of that technology can be exceedingly creative, and it hardly becomes those in advanced cultures, experiencing all of the benefits of technology, to decide that other cultures should be saved from its possible corruptions.

> Those who prate anti-technological nonsense in the name of some vague human values need to be asked "which humans?" To deliberately turn back the clock would be to condemn billions to enforced and permanent misery at precisely the moment in history when liberation is becoming possible. We clearly need not less but more technology.[8]

When we look at the implications of technology in private life, it is clear that technological expertise threatens to deny us any private life. The ability to miniaturize electronic "bugging" equipment means that conversations can be overheard by indetectible recording devices—the microphone in the olive in the martini glass is more than a paranoid joke, whereas the microphone installed in the telephone that works whether the phone is off the hook or not is already standard equipment for those who describe "law and order" as the highest good. The ability to transmit information into computer data banks means that there is instant information available about an individual at any time the government (or anyone else with access to the computer) wants it. Thus one's income tax record, banking habits, contributions to left-wing organizations, regularity in meeting alimony payments, make of car, size of mortgage, police record, and degree of support of the American Legion can be instantaneously and indiscriminately made available as a basis for deciding whether or not one should be

[8] A. Toffler, *op. cit.*, p. 350.

allowed to cross the Canadian border or continue to use his Master Charge card.

A discussion of what technology makes possible in the realm of biological research introduces a further set of problems, for the results can be both morally appalling and morally appealing. It is already feasible to implant electrodes in the brain to which impulses can be fed from outside so as to produce instant lust, instant passivity, instant hunger, or instant anger. Alternatively, a similar technique may be helpful in finding a cure for Parkinson's disease or training a stroke victim to regain the use of various body functions. On another level, we are closer and closer to the "cyborg," a fusion of organism and machine in an interrelationship so exquisite that neither can function without the other. A small preview of this is the space suit—an extension of, and refinement of, the astronaut inside it. The space suit is of no use without the astronaut. But the astronaut is of no use in space without the space suit. The same relationship exists between polio victims and the iron lungs that keep them alive.

As we are able to simulate more and more organs of the human body, the time will come when a "person" could have an artificial heart, artificial kidneys, artificial liver, and artificial limbs, thus becoming less and less distinguishable from a machine. Extraordinarily complex problems are raised by our increasing ability to weed out bad genes, preserve sperm in deep-freeze conditions for artificial insemination in the future, and control and manipulate the genetic code. There may come a time when we can achieve human reproduction by "cloning," in which exact duplicates of existing individuals can be asexually produced an indefinite number of times.

The realities and the possibilities discussed above have all sorts of scary implications as well as beneficent ones, and the scare factor is squared when one moves from the scientific questions to the humanistic questions: Who will control the controllers? What criteria will they use to decide which traits the genetic code should eliminate or accentuate? Who decides whether we clone Tillichs or Torquemadas? Will Daniel Berrigans be allowed to exist if Spiro Agnews are making the decisions? [9]

[9] For a fuller discussion of some of the issues raised in this section, see I. Barbour, *Science and Secularity: The Ethics of Technology* (New York: Harper & Row, 1970).

Can we make projections for the future?

Part of the difficulty in answering such questions has to do with the increasing difficulty in making projections for the future. The fact that experts with similar data come to astonishingly dissimilar conclusions does not enhance the confidence of the amateur that he can contribute anything useful. Nevertheless, two points germane to our discussion must be examined: [10]

One, the appearance of the "new" or unexpected can upset all our projections for the future. In *The Structure of Scientific Revolutions*, Thomas Kuhn points out that the development of a new "paradigm," or model of interpretation, can so alter our way of looking at our situation that a high degree of discontinuity is introduced. Many of the ways of thinking that were appropriate to an old paradigm do not carry over to a new situation, and what does carry over has to be rethought from a new perspective. The confidence with which we project the distant future out of our present paradigms is in itself a denial of the degree to which new paradigms may emerge along the way. We discover that we have taken up a parochial stance from which only the rude shock of new discoveries can release us—and yet the unexpected nature of the new discoveries simply underlines how futile would have been our attempts to anticipate them.

This appears to be so not only on the scientific-technological frontier, but on the sociological frontier as well. Until recently, for example, we have been schooled to deal with "the organization man," the easily recognizable individual who gives ultimate allegiance to the corporation. But we are now making the unanticipated discovery that allegiance to the corporation is a sometime thing. Alvin Toffler contrasts old-style bureaucracy with new style "ad-hocracy," in describing the astonishing mobility of top management people. Not only does the internal structure of any large organization change every year or two, but individual allegiances are instantly transferable, not only from Seagram to Calvert, but from Palmolive to Gen-

[10] Cf. the initial study by the World Council of Churches, *From Here to Where? Technology, Faith and the Future of Man* (Geneva: W.C.C., 1970).

eral Motors. The adjective that describes both the organization and the organization man is "temporary."

This and similar illustrations point up the high degree of the unexpected and, consequently, the need for modesty in projecting the future, at the very time when projections for the future are necessary if we are to avoid decisions that lead to less control over future uses of technology.

Two, this leads to a companion problem, which arises because the experts in a field do not, or cannot, establish adequate criteria to weigh the consequences of a development. In the burgeoning descriptive material on the technological era, there is astonishingly little reflection on such questions as Is this desirable? and even less on the more fundamental question, By what criteria do we determine that something is desirable? Either the values are considered implicit, or they are expressed with little apparent concern for whether they are appropriate values or not. B. F. Skinner is forthright in his *Beyond Freedom and Dignity* that both freedom and dignity have been overrated and that it is pointless to press for their retention. Many other planners seem persuaded that "freedom" is an illusion or a detriment to progress and that "individualism" is a throwback to outmoded frontier situations. If it can be argued that such values as freedom and individuality have flourished in societies that stressed pluralism and decentralization, it can further be argued that since technological society flourishes on homogeneity and centralization a fundamental conflict will have to be faced in the near future. Either the "old" values will have to be subordinated in the new era, or ways of preserving them in the new social and technological structures will have to be found. At the very least, the old problem of relating "freedom and order" emerges with special poignancy at a time when "order" is the increasing *sine qua non* for keeping the technological society functioning efficiently.

Even without insisting that freedom and individualism are to be highly valued, it can be insisted that "personhood" is increasingly endangered today and that too little attention is being given to its survival, let alone its growth, by those who project the technological future. And yet, the dilemma remains: Can one "plan" for the survival of human freedom without destroying the very thing one is trying to preserve?

Seeing the world in new ways

How can Christians relate to this bewildering new world about which they know so little and need to know so much? Where do they look for help? There is a great temptation to choose one of the experts and be guided by him. We can let Fuller provide examples of how the *imago dei* is being newly reflected in persons as partners in the ongoing process; or we can let Ellul reconvince us that sin is not only here to stay but has won the day at last; or we can wallow in the ambiguities we have already explored (a favorite theological posture) and do little more than throw up our hands, either in despair or prayer. Instead of choosing one of these tempting alternatives, we will first try to see how the frontier of technology can reorder some of our own Christian perspectives and then look at some ways in which the church can contribute to the living of frontier life in this area. There are at least four ways in which our Christian perspectives need reordering:

1. Most earlier attempts to deal with the person and the world have involved Christians in the triadic relationship God, self, and neighbor.[11] It has been insisted that no one of these roles, or indeed no two of them, can be understood without the third. Self and God are not fully understood unless the neighbor is involved (which is the basis for ethics), whereas self and neighbor are not fulfilled unless God is involved (which is the basis for a theological rather than a humanistic perspective). But the by-products of the technological revolution make us aware that more attention must now be given to the relationship between man and nature. We must now emphasize a *quadrilateral* rather than a triadic relationship, one that involves self, neighbor, God, and *nature*, or, in terms of the above discussion, self, neighbor, God, and the total environment—the environment that we can now control to some degree, which is also the environment that, if improperly controlled, can spell our destruction.

This was not emphasized in the past, at least by classical Protestant theology, because history rather than nature was

---

[11] Cf. *inter alia*, W. Beach and H. R. Niebuhr, *Christian Ethics* (New York: Ronald Press, 1955).

emphasized. (There may have been an analogous imbalance in eastern religions that have emphasized the triadic relationship of self, God, and nature, to the neglect of neighbor.) Thus, one of the things that Christians must acquire as they live on the technological frontier is a new affirmative stance toward nature, one that sees nature as comprising the entire environment, including the technological environment.

2. This would mean a new emphasis on the doctrine of creation and our relationship to it, not only on the created order that is "given" to us (the emphasis in classical theology), but also on our creativity within that order, involving a new spelling out of ways in which our increasing ability to manipulate the natural order through technology offers both promise and peril. In theological terms, this involves a fresh look at the relationship between creation and covenant. Karl Barth made a promising start in this direction in *Church Dogmatics* (III/1), but the effort is somewhat vitiated for our present purposes by the fact that creation is there viewed as the passive or inert "stage" on which the human drama is enacted. Such a view does not make sufficient allowance for the "interface" between ourselves and our environment, in which the relation between them is seen as a two-way street. The environment is clearly more than a set of stage props, and corrections to traditional ways of Christian thinking on this point can be drawn both from the writings of Teilhard de Chardin and contemporary "process theologians."

3. The new approach would involve more emphasis on a sacramental view of life, since this too would help break down sharp distinctions between ourselves and our environment and would ensure that the environment have a quality of the sacred about it. Materials and methods for such a new appreciation are already present in the church, and some of them will be discussed in the concluding chapter. We will anticipate that discussion only to the extent of suggesting that it should not be too difficult to extend the connection between recognizing the presence of God in bread and wine to recognizing his presence in all the other things that bread and wine symbolize—the agricultural and manufacturing processes that produce bread, the political and economic processes that make possible the distribution of bread, the sociological processes that help determine who gets bread and who does not, and the

technological processes that could ensure for the first time that no one need be without bread.

4. The frontier of technology necessitates an extensive rethinking of the so-called Protestant work ethic. In the past this ethic dictated that a person's worth was determined by a person's contribution to society. What the person "did" scored ethical points before other persons and before God. But on the technological frontier it will increasingly be the case that machines will do many of the jobs persons now do, and it will no longer be possible to achieve either outward recognition or inward satisfaction by the quantifiable methods of measurement used in the past. We will move from an ethic of work toward an ethic of leisure. This will entail new problems: How will we use our time when we no longer have to earn our living by the sweat of our brows and when the basic necessities of life can be assured to us without great effort to get them? What will we do when even a string of TV football games spread over a four-and-a-half day weekend begins to pall? What will we do with the guilt incurred by our belief that we are receiving "something for nothing"?

But that is only part of the problem. For a long time such an "ethic of leisure" will be a luxury possible only for a minority in the very rich nations. The leisure thus achieved will derive in part from the exploitation by the few of the many, a world where the most primitive methods of earning a livelihood still condemn the majority of the human family to lives at a starvation level. Is it likely to be the case that only the incentive of the "work ethic" can induce poorer nations to begin to compete for world markets? If it is not, can the necessary technological development be attained without cutting so seriously into the affluence of the richer nations that the "ethic of leisure" will have to be postponed indefinitely? To put the last question more bluntly: Is not the increasing prosperity of the United States liable to render it less open, rather than more open, to the plight of the rest of the world? Perhaps the rethinking must be even more extensive than we first assumed.[12]

---

[12] For a further discussion of these themes cf. I. Barbour, ed., *Earth Might Be Fair: Reflections on Ethics, Religion, and Ecology* (Englewood Cliffs: Prentice-Hall, 1972).

Relating the church to the new frontier

In what kinds of ways can the church begin to live on the technological frontier? It is too early for answers, but some suggestions can be made.

1. To anticipate an image developed in Chapter 8, as the church's numbers diminish and it becomes less beholden to establishment powers-that-be, the church could become a paradigm of a counter-culture using the tools of technology in a way that would avoid the dehumanization that can so easily follow technological advance. If the church, for example, became that arena in which people were consciously trying to embody Isaiah's vision of peace, and seeking a corporate style of life in which the modern equivalent of turning swords into ploughshares was being attempted, it might make contributions far out of proportion to what establishment-type thinking usually anticipates as possible.

2. As Robert Theobald has pointed out, there will be vast social changes in the technological future, but "this recognition of the problems of securing social change does not provide us with the right to place the need for social change above the personal needs of the human beings with whom we work." [13] If depersonalization turns out to be the greatest single threat in the future, it can be strongly argued that the church has the special role of warning about this and safeguarding the personal dimension against encroachment in the name of efficiency, progress, or technological necessity. The church could furthermore set itself to be that community in which personhood remained more important than "thing-hood," in the midst of a culture that is tempted to reverse those priorities. It might even assume the role of "technological ombudsman" that Toffler says society now desperately needs. And no matter how "new" the situation, it can keep posing the "old" questions that will persist in the "new" situation: Who will direct the planners? What are the criteria for determining that it is better to go in direction x than in direction y?

Donald Michael suggests that in our planless or overly planned plunge into the future we will need more than ever to have "external critics of institutions":

[13] In C. P. Hall, ed., *Human Values and Advancing Technology* (New York: Friendship Press, 1967), p. 47.

The point is that, so far as I can make out, the church and the theatre are the only two existing institutions of the society that are not immediately perceived by everybody as totally corruptible by the large system. Certainly you can't expect the sciences to play this role, or American philosophy, at least as we have known it in recent years. This role, this kind of external criticism, is absolutely crucial for responsible society.[14]

The fact that, as we have already noticed, little attention is given to the values that will determine our future, or to the kinds of controls that must be exerted over "the planners," suggests that the church must embody this role not only out of a long prophetic heritage, but also by the default of other social institutions.

3. The church may also have a responsibility to project, or at least to comment upon, scenarios for the future, based on its own doctrine of humanity. Granted that this will take technological expertise and that the wisdom of experts must be considered, it should be possible to react helpfully to various projections: beneficent scenarios, horrendous scenarios, scenarios that emphasize tight planning and control, and even scenarios that deny the possibility of scenarios. There is considerable wisdom accumulated over the prophetic centuries that has not become obsolescent in the light of technological breakthroughs.

This task is the more important since scenarios projected by those with political or economic power tend to become self-fulfilling prophecies. When scenarios emerge that depict us as conquerors of the earth, then the church must call attention to the pride involved in this picture and the dangers of using our power irresponsibly. When scenarios emerge that depict us as slaves of the machine, gradually diminished to the status of mere machines ourselves, then it will be necessary to call attention to certain depths of the human spirit that have emerged out of Jewish and Christian history that counterbalance such tendencies. If there are real possibilities, on the other hand, that we can become collaborators with the machine, then further attention must be given to the person-environment *interface* and ways in which it can ensure that the partnership

[14] *Ibid.* p. 104.

remains a partnership and not simply a step on the way to strangulation.

4. As the lines are more openly drawn between "rich" and "poor" nations, with an ethic of leisure possible for some only at the expense of backbreaking labor by others, the church will have to play the unpopular role of challenging the complacency of the affluent, reminding them that the earth is a "global village" in far more personalistic terms than McLuhan's use of that image suggests. Here a recognition that the church is not bound by nation, class, race, or geography may conceivably give it that measure of freedom not only to speak out about, but to begin to embody, the kind of society that could turn the technological frontier from a destructive nightmare into a healing vision.

6

The Frontier of Structures

If you are in a shipwreck and all the boats are gone, a
piano top buoyant enough to keep you afloat that comes along
makes a fortuitous life preserver. But this is not to say
that the best way to design a life preserver is in the form
of a piano top. I think we are clinging to a great many
piano tops in accepting yesterday's fortuitous contrivings
as constituting the only means for solving a given problem.
— R. Buckminster Fuller,
Operating Manual for Spaceship Earth, p. 9

Priest's secretary to priest arriving at work: "Two messages,
Father—the Bishop is quitting to get married and Sister
Celeste needs ten thousand dollars bail money."
— *New Yorker* cartoon

In one of those arresting ideas that the intellectually rich can
afford to elaborate in footnotes, Richard McBrien suggests that
it is time for the church to come to terms with the Einsteinian
revolution as well as the Copernican revolution.[1] The Copernican revolution was the recognition that the sun rather than
the earth was the center of the solar system. Father McBrien
insists that, analogously, this means that the Church must no
longer be viewed as the center of the history of salvation, but
must be replaced by the Kingdom of God.

Although this ecclesiastical counterpart of the Copernican
revolution has important implications for rethinking the matter of church structures, the analogy to the Einsteinian revolution is even more central. Where Copernicus had challenged
the heliocentric astronomy of Ptolemy, Einstein challenged the
assumption of Newton that "the laws of motion are the same
with respect to all inertial frames of reference."

[1] Cf. R. McBrien, *Do We Need the Church?* (New York: Harper &
Row, 1969), pp. 232-33, footnote 10.

Against the Newtonian assumption, Einstein posed the principle of relativity as a fundamental general law of physics. Space and time are not absolutes, but relative to the frame of reference of a particular observer. In our argument, *the structural components of the Church cannot be regarded as absolute in the Newtonian sense.* History itself is creative of new forms and the Christian community's consciousness of itself as the Body of Christ grows and matures in the context of progressive rather than static history.[2]

It is the perennial temptation to regard institutional "structural components" as "absolute," and, whereas there may be occasional historical moments when it is helpful to have an institution that appears to be unchanging, it is clear beyond any doubt that such an institution cannot thrive in a frontier situation.

Form follows function

Such a conclusion can be vindicated on a number of levels. It is an architectural maxim for example, that "form follows function." An architect does not create a structure and then ask whether or not it can be put to some use; instead, an architect is commissioned to make creative use of space for a particular function (the manufacture of beer, perhaps, or the worship of God); he then proceeds to develop a form appropriate to the fulfillment of the specified function. Thus, different functions will call for different forms, even the same function may be expressed in different forms in varying times and places. (A church in India may not have a heating system and one built in New York will not have a thatched roof.)

Similarly, Christians do not create a series of institutional structures — boards, bureaus, and bishops — and then ask whether or not they can be put to some use; instead, they are confronted with a need to proclaim and embody a certain truth (that God in his creative power has appeared in human life), and they subsequently develop structures to enhance the living and the spreading of that message. Once again, form follows function: the form of the church is dependent on the function of the church.

[2] *Ibid.,* pp. 232–33.

The point can be made theologically as well as architecturally. If the uniqueness of the Christian faith is a conviction about the uniqueness of Jesus of Nazareth, then we can take Herbert Butterfield's imperative at the conclusion of *Christianity and History* as a starting point: "Hold fast to Christ," Professor Butterfield writes, "and for the rest be totally uncommitted." [3] If that overstates the case, it nevertheless overstates it in a way that is helpful in thinking about church structures: those structures that are not expendable are those that help us to "hold fast to Christ"; those structures are expendable that do not. As Benjamin Reist puts it:

> The Church's sole reason for its being is to bear witness to Jesus Christ its Lord, in and to the world. All other things which are necessary parts of its existence—its government, its orders, its power, its sacraments—are subservient to this. [4]

At one time in history a hierarchical structure of church government may have been the best way to express this truth. The correspondence between priestly-papal authority and the civil authority of the feudal lord may have spoken powerfully to the medieval peasant about the ordering of his life. But that is no guarantee that such authority structures will communicate the same truth in another historical or cultural situation; if the current ferment in Roman Catholicism between the centralized authority of the Vatican and the decentralization of authority to national and regional bodies means anything, it means that the older structures have become a hindrance rather than a help.

The expendability of structures and the necessity of structure

The lesson is clear that specific structures are expendable, and that one of the great shortcomings of the church has been studied resistance to this fact. In recent years there has been a mouthfilling phrase in the ecclesiastical marketplace describ-

[3] H. Butterfield, *Christianity and History* (London: Bell, 1950), p. 146.
[4] In R. M. Brown and D. H. Scott eds., *The Challenge of Reunion* (New York: McGraw-Hill, 1963), p. 181.

ing this resistence: "morphological fundamentalism," i.e., fundamentalism or rigidity about the *morphē* (the form or structure) of the church. That which now is, presumably always was, and surely always shall be. But a quick catalogue of the structures of most contemporary congregations can join the issue: Sunday School, choir, paid ministry, buildings, denominational affiliation, women's auxiliary, budget. Many people would be tempted to say the church could not function without these. And yet it is an elementary fact of history that the church functioned for several hundred years without any of these. The structures, or certain structures at least, are clearly expendable.

But the argument can be pushed so far as to become self-defeating. For while it is clear that structures are expendable (and all the specific structures that have come and gone and remained in Christian history are in this category) it is quite another thing to say that no structure at all is necessary. Dietrich Bonhoeffer, writing to his godson on the occasion of the latter's baptism, prophesized that "By the time you have grown up, the form [i.e. structure] of the church will have changed greatly." [5] Bonhoeffer did not say that the church would have no structure, but only that it would have a different structure. Structures are expendable but structure is necessary.

There are two fundamental reasons why this is so: one is historical, the other theological. The historical reason is that with whatever change a new situation may demand, a sense of continuity is needed. Christian faith does not come into being *de novo* every day. It is a re-appropriation today of something that was also true yesterday and will also be true tomorrow, no matter how much the ways of stating or communicating it (i.e., the structures) may change. To the degree, for example, that Christianity is a communal faith, Christians will always gather together. But they need not always gather in buildings or gather only when ordained clergy are present to lead the gathering. When they gather, they will use some form to express what they are doing, but it need not be a Latin form, and the message they are communicating may sometimes be better expressed through dance than through

---

[5] D. Bonhoeffer, *Letters and Papers from Prison* (New York: Macmillan, 1972), p. 300. The German *Gestalt* can be translated as either "form" or "structure."

sermon. Nevertheless, there will be some kind of structure that joins them not only to one another but also to what came before, and it will communicate to whatever or whoever comes after.

There is a second, and allied, theological reason for the existence of some type of structure, even as specific structures are jettisoned or reformed. This is that the Christian affirmation itself is embodied in structural realities and can only be expressed through them. Christianity is not some sort of "spiritual" disembodied truth existing in a Platonized eternity, and attempts to make it such have sooner or later been condemned as heresy. The first major theological fight in the Christian community was over this very issue, initiated when certain groups tried to reduce Jesus to a principle or an eternal truth that only "seemed" (*dokeo* in Greek) to have participated in the flesh and blood reality of human existence. That Jesus could have lived, suffered, and died in the evil world of the flesh was anathema to them. The docetists lost in the face of the resounding affirmation that "the Word was made flesh and dwelt among us" (John 1:17). The very existence of Christian faith was dependent on structural embodiment in an earthbound human life.

Those who insist that Christian faith today can exist without corresponding structural embodiment are guilty of the same mistake, a mistake we can label "ecclesiastical docetism," i.e., a belief that the church can exist apart from any form or structure. If it is an error to believe that Christ can be present without any structure (e.g., specific, historical, concrete embodiment), it is likewise an error to believe that the church can be present without any structure (e.g., specific, historical, concrete embodiment).

So there must be structure, and the structure must be consistent with what is being communicated through the structure. But the minute we begin to equate what is communicated with the structure by which it is communicated, we are once again failing to take seriously both the Copernican and the Einsteinian revolutions.[6] Structure is necessary; structures are expendable.

[6] My own way of trying to make the point was to juxtapose on the title page of *The Spirit of Protestantism* (New York: Oxford University Press, 1961) the two verses: "Jesus Christ [is] the same yesterday, today and forever," and "We have this treasure in frail earthen vessels."

Three brief case studies

A random sampling of case studies in which certain structures of the church are being questioned makes the above discussion more specific.

1. In many quarters the residential congregation is under attack. Here is a structure, it is said, that has not only outlived its usefulness, but positively hinders the communication of the gospel, since the residential patterns of our communities reflect class, and often racial, segregation. If those near a given church attend it they simply reinforce, and appear to give divine sanction to, the discrimination that is such an ugly blight in the life of modern man.

The argument is extended by pointing out that the centers of decision-making are not in the suburban communities (where most residential churches are) but in the cities (where most residential churches are not). The church is thus out of touch with the currents of contemporary life, in the backwater rather than the main stream, the victim of what Gibson Winter has called "suburban captivity." So the question becomes: Must the parish perish?

It can scarcely be claimed that a residential parish is a *sine qua non* of the church, for the parish structure itself did not appear until the middle ages. Many examples of the church's presence in the world have nothing to do with residentially oriented congregations. But to say that the residential congregation is not an essential structure is not to say that it could not be one useful structure among others. If many people's lives are oriented around business in the city (for whom appropriate new types of church structure are necessary and are coming into being), there are others whose lives continue to be oriented residentially and to whom a ministry is still important. Indeed one of the most important insights that could come home to a residential congregation would be a recognition of the parochial nature of its own congregational life. This in itself could be a significant step toward enlarging the perspectives of those who might otherwise remain seated placidly on "comfortable pews."

Further, in the foreseeable future, residential congregations will continue to exist in considerable numbers, and they will continue to furnish the backbone of support for the other kinds of activities and structures with which the church must concern itself. There is the possibility of a creative interplay between the more conventional residential congregational structure and the *avant garde* structures that are emerging on the current scene. The local congregation, as a link between past and present, and as a point where many people are still within listening distance of the gospel, has an obligation and an opportunity to foster the kind of experimentation it may not itself feel ready to undertake. If it is not going to be among the *avant garde,* it should acknowledge that there are those within the church who must be, and should give both moral and financial support to those who are committed to "venturing far out" by means of new forms and structures.

This is a street, however, on which the traffic can run both ways. If *avant garde* projects can stimulate and challenge those within conventional congregations to a wider vision of the mission of the church in the world, the conventional congregations can provide to those within *avant garde* projects a sense of continuity, rootedness, and broad-based participation in the life of the whole church that is often not available to them. Thus, each can infuse the other with what is best in itself and purge from the other what should be discarded.[7]

2. A good deal has been said implicitly about the importance of *avant garde* experiments in the life of the contemporary church. Perhaps the most important thing to say explicitly is that experimental projects, churches, and ministries should always be viewed as provisional, coming into being in response to newly felt and unmet needs in the society to which the church ministers. The danger is to perpetuate such structures to vindicate the wisdom of the initial decision, even after they have passed the point of proven usefulness. A coffee house may have an institutional life of only eight months and still have been an important contribution at a given time in a changing neighborhood. A crash pad for drug addicts, a military counseling center, a ministry to jazz musicians, a "sanctuary" for men who must in conscience resist induction into the armed forces, a "house church" in an artist colony in a large city, a night ministry to "street people"—these and

---

[7] A slightly different approach to this problem can be found in the following chapter in the discussion of the religious "orders."

dozens of other experimental structures will come and go as the needs and unmet problems of modern life shift and vary. The church should be enthusiastic about initiating them and willing to terminate them when their usefulness has passed or to adapt them in new ways as other needs are perceived.

In R. Buckminster Fuller's analogy, the needs of the moment may call for the use of whatever materials are on hand, so that a piano top may serve as a temporary life-preserver. But that is only because the piano top rather than something else happens to float by. The church must be similarly flexible not only in meeting new crisis situations and in its choice of materials for meeting them most expeditiously and effectively, but also in its willingness to use different and possibly better materials as they come to hand.

A historical analogy for dealing with this problem is the story of the "church-related college" in America. In the early days of settlement, most churches established institutions of higher learning, initially to prepare men for "a learned ministry" and later to educate an informed laity. They saw that loving God with the mind necessitated training of the mind, and that, since no one else was doing the training, the church should. But before long, society as a whole began to assume responsibility for educating its constituency through the vehicle of public education, and any distinctive role for the church-related college (save as a place offering compulsory chapel and required religion courses) gradually disappeared. The demise of the church-related college should not be seen, however, as a defeat for the church, but as a triumph: the church did what society at first was not willing or able to do, and when society took up the task, the church was able to turn its resources and expertise in new directions.

Today's experiment becomes tomorrow's convention — or yesterday's folly. In either case, the church, having begun certain experiments can afford to let them be taken over by others or die a natural death.

3. There is one contemporary structure in the life of the church about which a certain "holy ruthlessness" is demanded. This is the structure of denominationalism. We have already argued that there was a time when denominations served the greater glory of God and were essential vehicles for bringing the gospel to the whole world. Most of them came into being to conserve and emphasize a part of the Christian message

that at that time seemed in danger of extinction or distortion. But because a structure was once needed is no guarantee that it is now needed, and the ongoing existence of denominations is a telling instance of "morphological fundamentalism." As was pointed out in Chapter 3, it can no longer be seriously argued that the message of justification by faith would disappear without Lutheranism; that the free pulpit is dependent on Presbyterianism; or that an ordered liturgy is uniquely co-extensive with Episcopalianism. Such emphases are no longer dependent on the institutional survival of the groups that gave them renewed expression at the time of the Reformation. So to argue is to remain locked into the past. Here is the area where institutional pride lingers longest and where vested interests employ the most powerful kinds of rationalization for what are often no more than self-serving ends. To settle for "spiritual unity" apart from some kind of visible unity is to succumb to ecclesiastical docetism and to deny that the message that "all are one in Christ Jesus" needs concrete historical manifestation.

To say these things, however, is not to say that there is a blueprint for one large united church in the future and that its translation into reality is the end of the road or will solve all problems. To assert that would make one guilty of equating the gospel with a particular structure or form. In working toward church reunion, as in all other things, it is crucial to remember that though structure is necessary, specific structures themselves are expendable. It may be that by the time divided Christian bodies have re-united another reformation will be required although a belief in "ongoing reformation" should make this unnecessary. But that is a problem for an age other than our own; surely our concern is to take whatever steps we can to heal the ugly wounds of division that have so marred the authentic presence of the Body of Christ in the world.[8]

The need to "travel light"

The church's problem in our day is not a lack of structures but a surfeit of them. We have not been plagued by formlessness,

[8] More detailed comments on the issue of reunion can be found in my *The Ecumenical Revolution* (Garden City: Doubleday, 1969), Chapter 8.

but by an overabundance of archaic forms for communicating the gospel that have become wrongly identified with the gospel itself. Faith in what is behind the institution very quickly becomes faith in the institution itself. And that is idolatry.

Much of the baggage that has been accumulated must be cast aside, and any new baggage that is acquired must be seen to be of temporary but by no means permanent usefulness. The preceding paragraphs and the succeeding chapters indicate some of the ways in which the church might learn to "travel light."

Hendrickus Berkhof once stated a single perspective that can be more useful than a dozen proposals. "I believe," he said, "that God is so humble that he decided to dwell in institutions; but we should know that they are more his manger and his cross than his temple."

This provides a realistic and self-correcting approach. The institutional church can be the "manger," the means by which God first encounters us in a most unexpected fashion; and it can be his "cross," the reminder that we destroy the one we first encounter in the manger. But the institutional church cannot be God's "temple"; it is not the place in which he really dwells, and its importance and value, however great, is always provisional. It is functional but not final. We need the constant reminder that John's vision of the new heaven and the new earth in the book of Revelation contains the startling statement, "I saw no temple there" (Revelation 21:22). This fact alone should make us humble about the inviolability of cherished church structures. In the final economy of God, the church will be no more.

When all is said and done, the important thing to remember is that the problem of structure is a secondary problem and not a primary problem. The primary problem is to have a vision of the church as an institution that needs structural embodiment, and then, and only then, seek out the appropriate structures by which, in a particular time and place but not for all times or all places, that vision can best be embodied. The most important thing is to discover images of the church that seem true. If they are, we can be sure that the structural materials to embody them can be found. Therefore, we are led to an examination of certain images for the frontier life of the church by an examination of structures.

7

Images for Frontier Life

There was a time when the church was very powerful—in the time
when the early Christians rejoiced at being deemed worthy to
suffer for what they believed. In those days the church was
not merely a thermometer that recorded the ideas and principles
of popular opinion; it was a thermostat that transformed the
mores of society.

—Martin Luther King, Jr., "Letter from
Birmingham Jail" in *Why We Can't Wait,* p. 91

Human beings always seek images to describe what is most
important to them. Martin Luther King, Jr., seeking to contrast a
docile culture-reflecting church with an active culture-changing
church, offers the constrasting images of a thermometer and
a thermostat. For the kind of task that faces us, images are
preferable to blueprints. Blueprints are self-defeating, since
they arrest a process of change and transform it into something fixed. Images, by contrast, suggest rather than stultify;
they open out rather than enclose; they present new ideas
rather than define old ones.

These are qualities essential to the living of frontier life,
where mobility and adaptiveness are prime requisites for survival and growth. It is a further requisite of frontier life that
what is appropriate in one time and place may be inappropriate in another. Thus, the ability to choose between a number
of images to define, for the moment, one's own existence, can
be a sign of growth rather than indecisiveness.

Our present task, therefore, is to examine a variety of images
of the church in order to see more clearly how frontier existence can be defined for our day. Those examined in this
chapter represent attempts to rehabilitate great images from
the past, while those in the following chapter are drawn from

contemporary human experience, as examples of an attempt to "hear the voice of God in the voice of the times." [1]

A controlling Jewish image: *Diaspora*

The obverse of the previously examined "Christendom" imagery, in which all are being gathered into the church, is *diaspora* or dispersion, in which Christians are being dispersed or scattered, throughout the world. The image of *diaspora* has the advantage of being descriptively accurate, theologically illuminating, and ecumenically appealing. Not only is it true that Christians are a minority scattered across the face of the world, but it can be argued that this is as it should be, and that for our day the image of the church in *diaspora* is the controlling image that other images can help clarify. It originates in the Jewish heritage all Christians share, and in our day has been explicated by churchmen as varied as the German Jesuit Karl Rahner; Hans-Reudi Weber, a former Swiss missionary to Indonesia now with the World Council of Churches; Richard Shaull, a former American Presbyterian missionary in Brazil now at Princeton Theological Seminary; Thomas Merton, a Cistercian monk who died on a trip exploring relations between Christianity and Buddhism; and Stephen Neill, an Anglican who became one of the first bishops of the Church of South India.[2]

---

[1] There is no intention of suggesting that these are the only images for our day, or that cumulatively they offer a full "doctrine of the church." Most of them have been written about before, but one is continually amazed at how what seems a commonplace to the expert can be a new and exciting discovery to others. For a fuller discussion of the Biblical material, cf. P. S. Minear, *Images of the Church in the New Testament* (Philadelphia: Westminster Press, 1960), where almost a hundred images and analogies are discussed.

[2] Cf. K. Rahner, *The Christian Commitment* (New York: Sheed and Ward, 1963), Chapter 1; Weber, "The Mark of an Evangelizing Church," in C. C. West and D. M. Paton, *The Missionary Church in East and West* (London: S.C.M. Press, 1959), pp. 101–16; R. Shaull, "The Form of the Church in the Modern Diaspora," in M. E. Marty and D. G. Peerman, eds., *New Theology No. 2* (New York: Macmillan, 1965), pp. 264–287; T. Merton, "The Christian in the Diaspora," in his *Seeds of Destruction* (New York: Farrar, Straus and Giroux, 1965), pp. 184–220; S. Neill, *The Unfinished Task* (London: Butterworth, 1957).

In spite of these impressive credentials, however, the image has been largely unnoticed by rank-and-file Christians, and, when noticed, it has usually been the object of apprehension since it challenges conventional ways of thinking about the church. We must therefore explore it with some care.

We can start with the descriptively obvious fact that Christians are a minority. This is obvious even in the centers of what was once called "Christian civilization," or "Christendom," and is painfully obvious when we include Asia and Africa. Even in what is presumably a "Catholic continent" such as South America, only a small number of people are truly committed to the church. As Richard Shaull puts it:

> Christendom is rapidly dissolving around us . . . without our going into exile, the non-Christian world has engulfed us as modern means of communication create one world in which we are a small minority, and as the population explosion indicates that each year the percentage of Christians decreases. We are thus in a situation similar to that of the Jews of the diaspora, scattered among people whose culture, mores and thought patterns are not like ours nor will they become so; our cathedrals and temples are no longer in the center of life nor do they bring the whole community together under God. If we hope to reach modern man, it will not be so much in terms of gathering him into the church as of going to him in the midst of our dispersion.[3]

As Shaull implies, this situation is "new" only in the sense that it is unlike the historical situation immediately preceding

---

Father Andrew Greeley, who is usually a good person to have on one's side, takes strong exception to the adequacy of the diaspora image. However useful it may be in Karl Rahner's Germany or in the third world, Father Greeley feels that "it does not serve as a useful tool in describing the position of the church in contemporary America ["Diaspora or Pluralism," *The Critic* (December 1965–January 1966), p. 56]. He counters that Christians are not a minority in the United States, and that the churches are not without influence. He does not believe that pluralism such as exists in the United States must mean diaspora, but that it can rather lead to "the denominational society," in which various religious bodies can contribute, compete, cooperate, compromise, and occasionally conflict with one another to the benefit of the total culture, and thus avoid the danger of any one of them becoming a new establishment.

[3] In M. E. Marty and D. G. Peerman, eds., *op. cit.*, p. 271.

it. But if we push back far enough we discover that the situation of the early church, and of the Judaism that preceded it, was also one of dispersion. The term was a common way of describing the Jews in the time of exile. When Palestine was overrun by a succession of world empire builders, the Jews found themselves scattered in all directions to such places as Egypt, Babylonia, Assyria, and Greece. The original "twelve tribes" were no longer together in Palestine, but in dispersion.

This parallels the situation of the early Christian community, and as Christians moved away from Jerusalem they duplicated the diaspora reality of their forebears. The Epistle of James is written "to the twelve tribes in the Dispersion" (James 1:1), or as the New English Bible puts it, "the twelve tribes dispersed throughout the world." First Peter begins with greetings "to the exiles of the Dispersion" (I Peter 1:1), rendered in the New English Bible as "God's scattered people." What happened was that little colonies of Christians sprang up in Corinth, Ephesus, Thessalonika, Athens, Colossae, and Rome. By the time of Constantine, the convictions of the handful had become the controlling religion of the majority, and "official Christianity" was on its way, leading to the establishment of a "Christendom" that was powerful for a millenium before the collapse that is so noticable in our day began. We are therefore once again back in the minority situation of the Jews in exile, scattered over the face of the non-Jewish world, and of the early Christians, scattered over the face of the non-Christian world.

In the face of all this, many Christians panic, and see their job as one of trying to regain lost territory, build up depleted church membership rolls, and Restore Ecclesiastical Influence in High Places. Their frenzy results from the mistaken assumption that the Christendom image is normative and that any departure from it points to the decline and fall of the Christian Empire. Here is where Karl Rahner, speaking to Roman Catholics, has words of wisdom for all of us.[4] He tells Catholics not to yearn wistfully for a past day, not to try to restore Roman Catholic Christendom, not to strive to win back power over the state. Rather than yearning for the past, Catholics

[4] Cf. K. Rahner, *The Christian Commitment* (New York: Sheed and Ward, 1963), Chapter 2, pp. 3–37.

should be affirmative about the present. The diaspora situation is no cause for despair; it is the situation in which God has placed Christians today, and they must consequently live the diaspora-life joyfully and affirmatively rather than seek to recapture the Christendom-life frantically and despairingly. The task is to discover new forms for the present era. Rahner takes seriously St. Augustine's statement, "Many whom God has the church does not have; and many whom the church has God does not have.[5] "Just where is it written," Rahner asks, "that we must have the whole hundred per cent? God must have all." [6] So there is no reason to assert that Christendom is the only possibility for the church. It may have fit an earlier culture, but it does not fit the present one.

Thomas Merton, writing in the context of a monastic vocation, seconds the motion and adds a further point of capital importance:

It seems to me that the meaning of the diaspora situation consists in recognizing this fact [e.g., that many outside the visible church are more full of the Spirit than those within] and in realizing how true it is that the Christian and the monk are actually living in a position of working out their own salvation and that of the world together with the non-Christian and the non-monk so that we actually have much to learn from them, and must be open to them, since *it is always possible that life-giving grace may come to us through our encounter with them.* This is what I mean by the Christian in diaspora. I am for the diaspora. I prefer it to the closed medieval hegemony. It may offer much better chances of a real Christian life and brotherhood.[7]

It is crucial to an understanding of diaspora to realize that Merton did not say that "life-giving grace goes from the Christian to the non-Christian," but that in the new diaspora situation the opposite can be true and that "it is always possible that life-giving grace may come to us through our encounter

[5] *Ibid.,* p. 35. Augustine elsewhere makes the point even more tersely, when he comments in talking about the visible church, "there are sheep without and wolves within."
[6] *Ibid.*
[7] T. Merton, *op. cit.,* p. 322; italics added.

with them." In a diaspora situation, then, Christians are not only dispersed throughout a non-Christian world, but are a listening as well as a speaking community, receiving as well as giving, and open to what is going on outside the church.

A threatening Biblical image: Going "outside the camp"

This matter of being "open to what is going on outside the church" is made clear in a Biblical image drawn from the Epistle to the Hebrews. Writing in the midst of the diaspora situation of the early church, when persecution was rapidly becoming commonplace, the author, instead of advising his readers to huddle together within the protective walls of the tiny fellowship, offers advice that is both surprising and threatening:

> Jesus also suffered outside the gate in order to consecrate the people through his own blood. *Therefore let us go forth to him outside the camp*, bearing abuse for him.[8]

The advice is surprising because the initial assertion is surprising. It reminds us that Jesus did not die within the gates of the holy city of Jerusalem in a religious atmosphere. He died outside the city wall, and he died a very secular death at the hands of the political authorities in a very secular place —the city dump heap, to be precise. To Christians who knew the history of their Jewish upbringing, the imagery of the camp was a clear way of describing the people of Israel who used to move their tents from day to day and who made camp each night. Only those who rebelled against God or his appointed leader were to be put outside the camp.[9] So Jesus, understood by the early Christians as the "Lord of the camp," is described as being found outside the camp. This is a way of saying that he was identified with the rebels and outcasts who had been excluded from the camp and that to find him one must go outside.

This is surprising indeed. But on examination it turns out

---

[8] Hebrews 13:12–13; italics added.
[9] Cf. Numbers 12 and the story of Miriam for an example.

to be even more threatening than surprising because, given this bit of information about where Jesus is to be found, the reader is also told to go outside the camp into the abode of the outcast. And just in case the point is not yet fully clear, the writer goes on to describe what existence outside the camp is like: it means "bearing abuse."

Where, then, is the Christian to look for God today? Only inside the church? Only within the security of the like-minded fellowship? No. God is at work outside the camp, and if one expects to find him, that is the place one must go. The Christian does indeed go inside the church, as subsequent images will make clear, but what he learns "inside" is that God is "outside" in the midst of the brutality and brokenness of life.[10]

The point has been made architecturally in the chapel of the Episcopal Theological Seminary of the Southwest in Austin, Texas. Sitting in the chapel, one is inescapably aware of the cross as the focal point of the building. The cross is an uncomfortably life-sized cross, rather than an aesthetically pleasing ornament. But the cross is not inside the chapel at all. It is outside the walls of the chapel, outside the camp, plainly visible through the large window behind the altar, but planted firmly in the world beyond, the world in which there is also a high-energy physics laboratory, a university, snarled city traffic, and slums. That is where the Christian drama is played out. That is the place to which the Christian is summoned.

A revamped medieval image: The religious orders

In any attempt to be relevant, the Middle Ages might seem the last place to turn, especially since they represent the high point of the Christendom imagery. And yet there is an experience out of the medieval period that provides a useful image for our own day. This is the image of the religious orders and the monastic communities. Before we dismiss them as anti-

---

[10] This approach could also be described (in the language of Chapter 4) as an attempt to discern God's pseudonymous activity in the world, the strange ways in which he is at work where men least expect him; and in Jesus as the pseudonym *par excellence*, the one who is "despised and rejected of men." A political execution is surely the last place one would expect the Lord of creation to be revealing himself.

quated "withdrawals from the world," let us look at what they represented.

Medieval Christians were aware that all was not well with the church; it had become corrupt, power-hungry, and rich. Some of them gave up on the church and left; others tried, with increasing frustration to "reform from within the existing structures"; still others, however, created new structures, but without totally abandoning the old ones. The new structures, the religious orders, had some continuity with the past, but they also provided a degree of freedom for experimentation and genuine renewal that had become impossible within the ordinary framework of the church. The Benedictines, despairing of the liturgical chaos of the times, established an order dedicated to liturgical experimentation and renewal. The Dominicans, appalled by the low state of scholarship in preaching, established a community called the Order of Preachers. The Franciscans, repelled by the wealth of the church, formed a brotherhood committed to living in holy poverty, in imitation of the Son of Man who had nowhere to lay his head. In a similar fashion, countless orders of nuns came into being, all with special tasks, such as teaching, nursing, caring for the elderly.[11]

For all their differences, the religious orders shared certain common characteristics:

1. They were founded in response to a particular need. A job needed doing, a job that for reasons of corruption, inefficiency, or lack of vision was not being done and apparently could not be done within the ordinary structures of the church. Consequently, a special group was formed to do the job.

2. While insisting on a great deal of freedom, mobility, and semi-autonomy, the orders remained part of the church universal. They did not try to "become new churches," but worked out ways to move in new directions within the existing church, in ways that not only met a particular need, but also had an impact on the life of the church.

3. Members of the religious orders lived under a discipline.

[11] It has been said that there are only three things God doesn't know. He doesn't know (a) what a Dominican doesn't know, (b) what a Jesuit really thinks, and (c) how many orders of nuns there are.

The terms of membership were far more strict than those of ordinary "church membership," usually involving the acceptance of the disciplines of poverty, chastity, and obedience. It was acknowledged that life must be lived under a certain discipline if the distinctive witness of the order was to be maintained.

4. In principle, at least, the orders were *ad hoc.* If the particular job an order created to do was done, or the particular reforms envisaged were achieved, it was ready to disband, content that its witness had been made and that the church to that degree had been purified so that it was no longer necessary to maintain the order. In practice, of course, the story was a different one. The orders tended to become solidified and static, they were more and more absorbed into the "establishment" and were less and less distinguishable as the *avant garde.*[12] But the principle is important: groups founded to do a particular job must consider themselves expendable when the job is done or, at the very least, flexible enough to find new jobs to do.

These four characteristics have great transfer value today. What the contemporary church needs today are some contemporary counterparts to the medieval religious orders, flexible structures that allow Christians to do jobs that need doing and yet operate with greater freedom and efficiency than seems possible within existing church structures. Let us look briefly to two examples that are different enough to counterbalance any lurking tendency to premature stereotyping.

For example; a group originally known as "Clergy and Laymen Concerned about Vietnam," is analogous to a medieval order. (1) The contemporary order came into being because a job needed doing. There was need for protest against an immoral war, protest that simply was not possible at the time within the cumbersome and timid denominational and ecclesiastical structures of main-line Christianity. (2) Those who formed the new group did not, for the most part, leave their own churches

---

[12] The obvious example is the Franciscans, who, within a generation of the death of a founder who had insisted that possessions were anathema, were well on their way to becoming one of the most affluent groups within the medieval church.

but remained within them. It can be argued that the strength given by the corporate witness of the order has not only had a gradually cumulative impact on public policy, but has also been a leaven, sensitizing the corporate conscience of the main-line churches. (3) The members of the order have committed themselves to a discipline. It has not been the three-fold discipline of poverty, chastity, and obedience, but it has been the discipline of giving much time and also much money to the order and its cause. Staff people have served on low salaries, and members have frequently given beyond their means. All have given enormous amounts of time. (4) The order is clearly *ad hoc*. It does not intend to become a church or any kind of permanent structure and when Vietnam ceases to be a "concern," the group can disband or it can become "concerned" about other issues arising out of all that Vietnam symbolized.[13] (5) A new characteristic of "Clergy and Laymen Concerned about Vietnam" does not derive from the medieval experience but is a contemporary input. This is the fact that from the beginning the contemporary order has been ecumenical as well, including not only Christians but Jews, along with "men of good will" who do not answer to any typical religious affiliation. Indeed, the widely used phrase "men of good will" is no longer inclusive enough, since this order also includes many women who are increasingly restive at being classed as men, and whose presence also illustrates that the sexual segregation of the medieval orders has been transcended in the new situation.

There are also more informal adaptations of the image of the religious order. These exist in the form of *ad hoc* groups who do not find their own needs sufficiently nourished and challenged by conventional, middle-class congregations. Members of these groups realize that they need "something more," and yet they are not ready to turn their backs on what even those middle-class congregations might become. Thus they involve themselves in two groups; on the one hand, they are members of First Presbyterian or All Souls Episcopal or St. Clement's Roman Catholic Church, but, on the other hand, they also meet from time to time with concerned Christians

---

[13] Since these lines were first written the name has been changed to "Clergy and Laity Concerned." Q.E.D.

drawn from all of those churches and perhaps others as well. They gather frequently or infrequently in someone's home, where many different things may happen. They may discuss what their common faith demands of them in relation to a School Board election or the draft refusal of their children. They may meet to pledge moral and tangible support to one another, so that if a member of the order loses his job for taking a political stand, he knows that the others will help him during the period of unemployment. Frequently they share a meal around the dining room table, a table on which there is usually bread and wine over which the familiar but ever-new words of institution are said and around which the giving of the "peace" may represent a truer communion than most of them experience on Sunday morning around another table.

There is a danger in such groups. It is the danger of self-righteousness or smugness, the feeling that only those within the group know "where it's really at." The fact that such groups cross ordinary denominational lines, however, is one safeguard against preciousness, as is the decision not to make the order an alternative to, but a supplement to, ongoing church life. However, even recognizing their potential danger, the hope must be that as such informal orders grow, there will be inter-actions between them and the congregations from which their members are drawn, so that congregations can be "radicalized" by those within the order, while those within the order can keep the sense of continuity and stability embodied in more conventional structures.[14]

---

[14] It may be worth noting that the writer as a Protestant has taken a Catholic model, whereas certain Catholic writers have taken the model of the Protestant sects to make the same point. [Cf., for example Rosemary Ruether, "The Free Church Movement in Contemporary Catholicism," in M. E. Marty and D. G. Peerman, eds., *New Theology No. 6* (New York: Macmillan, 1969), pp. 269–287.] The reasons for this difference reside, I believe, in the degree of importance attached to *continuity* within change. Many Cotholics have had all too much continuity of a sort that has been oppressive, so that the clean break that sectarianism represents is appealing. Protestants, however, need to be reminded that their great temptation has always been in the direction of "the clean break," the severing of roots with the past, and the mistaken notion that one can start *de novo*. Actually, not even the sect starts from scratch: it simply rejects the immediate past in favor of a more distant past.

A neglected Reformation image: The mark of mission

We have previously called attention to the significance of mission, or being sent forth, as a characteristic of Christian faith, in spite of the uneasiness that surrounds the term today.[15] It is now important to relate this theme more directly to the life of the church itself. We can begin by noting that mission as a mark of the church was neglected by the Protestant reformers and that this led to impoverishment in the understanding of the church.[16]

What are the marks of the church for the reformers? The answer is clear: the church is found "where the Word is truly preached and the Sacraments are rightly administered." Bracketing the question of how to weigh the crucial adverbs (*"truly* preached" and *"rightly* administered"), it is still clear that the definition is a description of the inner life of the community only.

Lacking in this sixteenth-century understanding of the church is any acknowledgment of the outreach or missionary concern of the church. Few people have argued this point so forcefully in our day as has Karl Barth in his *Church Dogmatics,* and since Barth's devotion to the reformers and their cause is beyond dispute, the critique he offers is particularly telling. In his development of the point, Barth deals with the church in three ways. He talks first about the gathering of the church, then about its upbuilding, and finally about the sending forth (i.e., the mission) of the church. He scolds the reformers for ignoring the latter point:

> What has become of the decisive New Testament saying in II Corinthians 5:19 that it was the world which God reconciled to Himself in Jesus Christ, or of the well-known John 3:16 that it was the world which He loved so much in such a way that He gave for it His only begotten son . . . . It was often maintained that on earth in this age the church has to fight not only against the flesh and the devil but also against the world. But above

---

[15] Cf. Chapter 2, "The Frontier of Mission."
[16] For what follows cf. *inter alia,* C. W. Williams, *Where in the World?* (New York: National Council of Churches, 1963), and K. Barth, *Church Dogmatics* (Naperville, Ill.: Allenson, 1969), IV/3, Part two, pp. 762–95.

all does it not have to exist for it? The fact that the Church exists for the world and not for itself does not appear at all . . . . Was it for this reason that in the 16th and 17th centuries the Protestant world was characterized by that pronounced lack of joy in mission, and even unreadiness for it? . . . . There can be no doubt that we are here confronted by a noticeable gap in the Evangelical dogmatic tradition.[17]

Barth contends that sending forth, or mission, is a necessary mark of the church and not an afterthought at the last minute or perhaps omitted altogether.

The true Church may sometimes engage in tactical withdrawal [from the world] but never in strategic . . . . In every respect, even in what seems to be purely inner activity like prayer and the liturgy and the cure of souls and Biblical exegesis and theology its activity is always *ad extra*. It is always directed *exira muros* to those who are not, or not yet, within, and visibly perhaps never will be.[18]

There are those today who feel that even with Barth's emendation, the Reformation marks remain antiquated and introverted. One could pursue this theme by suggesting that perhaps the contemporary marks should be such outward-oriented themes as faith, hope, and love and that where these are truly present we can believe that the church is present. Much of this is suggested by the images to which we now turn.

A disturbing Christological image: The servant church

How, then, does the church go forth outside the camp or *extra muros*, as Barth puts it? What is its posture? How does it

---

[17] K. Barth, *op. cit.*, pp. 766–67. Barth goes on to buttress his point with some very obvious Biblical support, e.g., "As my Father has sent me into the world, even so have I sent them into the world" (John 17:18).

[18] *Ibid.*, p. 780. Barth's use of the term *extra muros*, "outside the walls," indicates how the images we have been examining overlap in a mutually reinforcing way, recalling the imagery earlier drawn from the Epistle to the Hebrews.

embody such qualities as faith, hope, and love? There is one image that draws together such questions in a relevant and disturbing fashion. This is the image of the servant church, drawn from the New Testament description of Christ as servant. The terminology is familiar; the implications of the terminology are usually avoided.

It would be hard to fault the notion that there is a connection between Christ and the church and that what he stood for and did is what the church should stand for and do. This can be affirmed quite apart from such controverted questions as whether or not Jesus intended to found a church and whether or not he directly established particular forms of ministry or ecclesiastical organization. The Christian community grew up around allegiance to the person and work of Jesus, remembering him, knowing him still, anticipating his return to fulfill what he had begun, and charged in the interim with embodying the quality of life and ministry he had exemplified.

Different branches of the church and different eras of Christian history have modeled themselves on different aspects of Jesus' life and ministry. The period of Christendom, for example, saw Jesus as conqueror, *pantocrator,* the one who reigns over all. However, the church of this period made a disasterous univocal transfer of its imagery from Christ to the church, asserting that if Christ rules over the world the church also rules over the world. Forgotten was the fact that Christ also rules over the church, so that the church can never be more than the servant of the true ruler.

This brings us full circle to the image most appropriate in a time of diaspora, for even images of Jesus as victor must cope with the reality that any victory Christians speak of comes through humiliation and apparent defeat; the cross may not be bypassed or ignored. Thus the Christological imagery most appropriate for diaspora existence will be the imagery of Christ as servant, and even more as suffering servant. "Even the Son of Man," Jesus tells his followers, "did not come to be served, but to serve." (Mark 10:45, N.E.B.)

The Pauline stress on Jesus' self-emptying (*kenosis*) is the Christological stress most needed at present, and Paul uses it explicitly as a model for church life in Philippi:

Let your bearing towards one another arise out of your life in Christ Jesus. For the divine nature was his from the first; yet he did not think to snatch at equality with God, but made himself nothing, assuming the nature of a slave. Bearing the human likeness, revealed in human shape, he humbled himself, and in obedience accepted even death—death on a cross.[19]

So much may sound almost trivially familiar. It is therefore useful to recall that Dietrich Bonhoeffer gave a contemporary restatement of this theme in his description of Jesus as "the man for others," the one whose presence in the world is not for his own sake, but for the sake of the brethren. The important point in the present discussion is the corollary Bonhoeffer drew: if Jesus is the man for others, and the church is to continue his mission, then the church must be "the church for others," the community whose presence in the world is not for its own sake, but for the sake of the neighbor, meaning by "neighbor" the whole human family. In his "Outline of a Book," Bonhoeffer indicates what this might mean:

The church is the church only when it exists [i.e., is there] for others. To make a start, it should give away all its property to those in need. The clergy must live solely on the free-will offerings of their congregations, or possibly engage in some secular calling. The church must share in the secular problems of ordinary human life, not dominating, but helping and serving. It must tell men of every calling what it means to live in Christ, to exist for others.[20]

It is worth noting that the recovery of the servant image is not limited to individual theologians writing out of extraordinary circumstances. It is also being recovered in more official ways by established church bodies. Two examples will

---

[19] Phil. 2:5-8, N.E.B.
[20] D. Bonhoeffer, *Letters and Papers from Prison*, new, greatly enlarged edition (New York: Macmillan, 1972), pp. 382-83. It should be remembered that Bonhoeffer was writing in the situation of a state church in Germany that received direct financial aid from the state. Thus in his own context the suggestions were even more alarming to satisfied churchmen.

illustrate the point. The first is an explicit reappropriation of the image by Vatican II:

> Inspired by no earthly ambition, the Church seeks but a solitary goal: to carry forward the work of Christ Himself under the lead of the befriending Spirit. And Christ entered this world to give witness to the truth, to rescue and not to sit in judgment, to serve and not to be served.[21]

The theme was symbolized by Cardinal Léger, archbishop of Montreal, who left his post of great power after Vatican II to serve lepers in an African mission colony.

A second example is contained in the Confession of 1967 of the United Presbyterian Church in the U.S.A.:

> The life, death, resurrection and promised coming of Jesus Christ has set the pattern for the church's mission. His life as man involves the church in the common life of men. *His service to men commits the church to work for every form of human well-being.* His suffering makes the church sensitive to all the sufferings of mankind so that it sees the face of Christ in the face of men in every kind of need. His crucifixion discloses to the church God's judgment on man's inhumanity to man and the awful consequences of its own complicity in injustice. In the power of the risen Christ and the hope of his coming the church sees the promise of God's renewal of man's life in society and of God's victory over all wrong.
>
> The church follows this pattern in the form of its life and in the method of its action. So to live and serve is to confess Christ as Lord.[22]

It cannot be denied that when one looks at the American church today the image of servanthood seems ridiculously inappropriate in the midst of huge budgets, air-conditioning, and gospels of success. This, however, is the reason not to discard the image but to insist on it more strongly, for the image must persist as the fully authentic goal of Christian existence; an

---

[21] W. M. Abbot, ed., "The Church Today," *Documents of Vatican II* (New York: Association Press, 1966), p. 201.

[22] Cited in E. A. Dowey, Jr., *A Commentary on the Confession of 1967 and an Introduction to the Book of Confessions* (Philadelphia: Westminster Press, 1968), p. 19, italics added.

ongoing recognition of the disparity between the image and the actuality may be important leverage in getting the church back to a more authentic churchmanship.

There is a further aspect of the servant imagery that can be highlighted by exploring a dilemma. The theme of servanthood places a high premium on reconciliation: a church that is not trying to dominate but to serve will be a vehicle through which those who do seek to dominate may be persuaded to be reconciled.[23] Since God was in Christ reconciling the world to himself, the ongoing task of reconciliation is the way in which the servant church will seek to serve the world.

But things get complicated when we recognize that another demand upon the church today is to take sides, to become the advocate of the dispossessed.[24] This too is a function of the servant church, for a servant church must identify with the servants in society, particularly the oppressed servants, rather than the masters. If the church must become the church of the poor rather than of the rich, will this not lead to increased conflict rather than reconciliation?

We must remember that reconciliation is not the absence of conflict, but a way of dealing with conflict and of indicating what can lie on the other side of conflict. If there is injustice, reconciliation can hardly consist in maintaining the *status quo* to avoid conflict, for the injustice will persist. Reconciliation will have to involve ways of overcoming the injustice so that there can be genuine rather than spurious reconciliation. When the forces of injustice have enough power to perpetuate oppression, the servant church will be denying its servanthood unless it sides with the oppressed. It may be clear what this would involve in the third world where the lines between "oppressed" and "oppressor" are clearly drawn; it may be less clear what this would involve in America, where the structures of society that oppress certain groups tend to be just those structures that benefit white, middle-class churches. Without ceasing to

---

[23] It is significant that the overall theme of the Confession of 1967, from which an extended quotation about servanthood was given above, cites reconciliation as the key theme needing emphasis in the life of the church today. The same point has been stressed in Catholic theology; cf. E. C. Bianchi, *Reconciliation: The Function of the Church* (New York: Sheed and Ward, 1969).

[24] Cf. the discussion of this theme in Chapter 4, "The Frontier of Revolution."

minister to the privileged (who are also God's children) could the church through that ministry bring the privileged to see how much their privileges are purchased at the expense of the rest of humanity? There could hardly be a more threatening question, since no group of people (not even church people) is ever prone to relinquish privilege voluntarily. Thus, the attempt to reconcile will produce conflict not only between the church and the society around it, but within the church as well.

This is why the servant image was initially described as a disturbing one. But unless such problems can be openly faced and worked through, all brave talk about the church for others will be no more than hyperbole and hypocrisy.

8

More Images for Frontier Life

God writes straight with crooked lines.
—Charles Péguy

We have examined five images drawn from past frontier situations that can be adapted creatively to our present frontier situation. We now turn to appropriate some images drawn from the contemporary scene. Some of these were initiated in areas of life far from ordinary church life, whereas others come out of contemporary church experience. All of them illustrate the truth that many resources in addition to conventional resources are available, which is only another way of agreeing with Péguy that God writes straight with crooked lines.

A unifying ecumenical image: Summoning and sending

Our attention to the outward-oriented life of the church may seem to have destroyed the notion that the church has an inner life as well. It will therefore be appropriate to begin with an ecumenical image that has received attention in discussions sponsored by the World Council of Churches, in which the church is described as gathering and dispersing or summoning and sending. The tendency in the past was to stress summoning, the church as the community that gathers together. (*Ek-klesia* means those who are "called out" from the world.) What is now being stressed is sending, which must be understood as an integral part of summoning: the church is summoned for the sake of being sent. This has been true since the beginning. The marks of the summoned church in Acts 2:42—teaching, fellowship, breaking of bread, and prayer—

were set in the context of the apostles being sent into the world. Throughout Luke-Acts, Jerusalem is the point of gathering for the disciples, but it is also the point of departure in going forth "to all the nations." If it was the place to which they came, it was also the place from which they went.[1]

The value of contemporary recovery of the summoning-sending imagery is to remind us that if "being sent" is not the whole story, neither is "being summoned." Each needs the other and the rhythm of their relationship is captured in the comments of a World Council of Churches working committee:

> [The] people of God is gathered from all peoples, cultures and groups of society, in order to be scattered again. Therefore, *the scattering of the Church is as important as the gathering of the Church.* Only through its dispersion can the church function as the salt of the earth. Only through its scattering can the Church be present in the world where the real battles of faith are fought. We do not ignore the deep significance of the appearance of the Church when it is gathered; indeed, this gathered community is a mighty token of the communion of Saints, rendering praise to God on behalf of the world which is still scattered. But we would like to stress the fact that the gatherings of the Church must also be seen and shaped in the view of the scattering of the Church. Because, during this time between Christ's ascension and return, the Church lives and works essentially as a "community of the dispersed." Only if we recover that Biblical rhythm between gathering and scattering can our churches become what they are meant to be: evangelistic communities, the salt of the earth.[2]

We can sum up the interrelationship of summoning and sending in three interconnected and cumulative propositions:
The church is the summoning community. It summons men

---

[1] Cf. further on these points, J. R. Nelson, *The Criterion for the Church* (New York: Abingdon, 1961).

[2] Cited in H. J. Margull, *Hopes in Action* (Philadelphia: Muhlenberg Press, 1962), p. 191; italics added. Cf. also H. R. Weber, *Salty Christians* (New York: Seabury Press, 1963); and A. Toynbee, *A Study of History* (London: Oxford University Press, 1934–39); who has made extensive use of a similar theme under the rubric of "withdrawal and return."

to hear its message, to enter it, and to become a part of its fellowship. Its message and its life center around Jesus of Nazareth, defined (in various ways) as one who embodied in a fully human life the presence of God on the human scene. One who responds to the summons usually enters the community by baptism, signifying the washing away of the past and a new beginning. Such a person continues life in the fellowship through participation in the holy communion, a meal of thanksgiving that celebrates the possibilities for new life in company with this same Jesus, present in the midst of those who gather around his table. The respondant also makes a commitment to the fellowship, hoping to be a channel through whom the love God has offered there can be poured out on others. Therefore:

The church is summoned for the purpose of being sent. Its be-all and end-all is not the establishment of a cosy and intimate fellowship of the few, but the transformation of summoning love into sending love. It is not just the place to which people come but also the place from which they go. The church is to be turned inside out, so that what is true within also becomes true without, so that what is ideally true around the Lord's Table really becomes true around every other table, i.e., mutuality, sharing, and love.

The church is sent to embody the love it has received. If persons receive love in the summoning, they are to share love in the sending. If they learn about justice in church, they are to embody justice in the office building. If they discover that God does not differentiate between races around a Lord's Table, then they are not to differentiate between races around a restaurant table.[3]

---

[3] The ecumenical image is given an even greater ecumenical range, by referring to Martin Buber's treatment of revelation. Buber, a Jew, describes revelation as both summons and sending, as both a calling and a mission. The call is not an end in itself; it is for the purpose of mission: "The encounter with God does not come to man in order that he may henceforth attend to God but in order that he may prove its meaning in action in the world. All revelation is a calling and a mission [German: *Berufung und Sendung*] . . . . When you are sent forth, God remains presence for you; whoever walks in his mission always has God before him: the more faithful the commandment, the stronger and more constant the nearness." [M. Buber, *I and Thou* (New York: Scribners, 1971), p. 164.]

A contemporary sociological image:
The church as a "counter-culture"

Much attention is being given to the emergence of a "counter-culture," typified by individuals or small groups who have repudiated the values or the institutions surrounding them and are developing alternate life styles. In their affirmation of the new, they engage in repudiation of the old, in ways that may range from the adoption of distinctive hair styles to modes of communal living that challenge the old style nuclear family. Politically the counter-culture can range from radical politics to apolitical postures; technologically it can run the gamut from disavowal of television to affirmation of hi-fi stereo. When asked why they do not work within the system, practitioners of the counter-culture respond that the system has infinite resources for absorbing dissent without accepting its challenge and of tolerating non-conformity just enough to neutralize its imperative for change. In Theodore Roszak's imagery, the culture surrounding us today is "a capacious sponge able to soak up prodigious quantities of discontent and agitation, often well before they look like anything but amusing eccentricities or uncalled-for aberrations." [4]

The counter-culture *motif* is thus a repudiation of the idea of gradual reform-from-within and an attempt of a few to embody now the kind of life that ought to be possible for all. Just as a movie preview tells us enough about the coming attraction so that we want to see the full-length feature, so the expression of the counter-culture tries to embody a preview of coming attractions. The new style is still not present in full force, but enough of it is present to show others what the full-fledged experience would be like and to persuade some of them to adopt the new life style themselves.

This imagery is full of potential meaning for the church, and could have great attractiveness for those who feel that the church has also been co-opted by the culture or allowed

---

[4] T. Roszak, *The Making of a Counter-Culture* (New York: Doubleday-Anchor, 1969), p. xiv. Herbert Marcuse makes the same point in a discussion of the "repressive tolerance" of a so-called democratic society, in R. P. Wolff, B. Moore and H. Marcuse, *A Critique of Pure Tolerance* (Boston: Beacon Press, 1968), pp. 81–123.

just enough repressive tolerance to blunt, if not neutralize, its concern to transform the world around it. To many people, American Protestantism is no more than "the Republican Party on its knees," or a Sunday version of the Rotary Club. The "sermons preached at the White House" turn out to be religious justifications of the political stance of the White House incumbent totally without critique or prophetic challenge.

But the church is not meant to mirror the culture around it. In an impersonal, technological, manipulative era it is called upon to emphasize the person, to point out that a technology that produces napalm needs to be transformed, to offer an alternative to manipulative techniques. It is meant, in other words, to be a counter-culture, to offer a "more excellent way," to be a preview of coming attractions, to embody an alternate life style that can demonstrate how life can be creatively lived right now and not only in the distant future. It is to be the place where people can, in Thoreau's over-used and under-practiced phrase, "march to the beat of a different drum." [5]

It may sound as though the counter-culture image were identical with that of the religious orders. But while the overall intent is similar, the counter-culture image is more radical. The image of the religious orders is a model for some within the church to transform the church, whereas the image of the counter-culture is a model for the entire church to transform the world. To step from the acceptance of the values in one's culture to the acceptance of a new set of values that will challenge that culture, is no small step but a gigantic one; changing one's pace to adapt to the beat of another drum may be so disjunctive as to deserve the name conversion, which literally means turning around, facing in a new direction.

There are at least two ways, then, that the image of the counter-culture could contribute to a new understanding of the church today. The first of these sees the church as the locus for alternate life styles: the "preview" community in which

[5] The theme has been developed in more conventional theological terminology by such Catholic theologians as Karl Rahner and Edward Schillebeeckx who describe the church as "the sacrament of the Kingdom of God," the place where what God has in store for all his people is already embodied in the here and now. It has been extended to the even bolder but more difficult imagery of the church as "the sacrament of the world."

here-and-now mutual support replaces destructive competition, in which people share with one another instead of being fearful of one another, in which love of God leads to love of neighbor and love of neighbor embodies love of God. The church becomes the place in which people say "yes" to a set of values usually considered hopelessly visionary.

But in addition to this affirmation of new values, the church as a counter-culture could challenge old values through an embodiment of the life of creative dissent. Contemporary society needs to be challenged, not only because of the hollowness of its values, but also because it seeks to curb dissent in an increasingly heavy-handed way, challenging the integrity and legitimacy of those who march to the beat of a different drum.

The church began as a counter-culture, and its most creative times in a checkered history have been those times when it sought to re-assume that role. Because it says "yes" to its own distinctive allegiances, it must say "no" to other allegiances that the culture or the state tries to impose upon it. It will help to recall some historical examples: [6]

The basic ingredient for the counter-culture stance is shared with Judaism. Jahweh says to his people, "You shall have no other gods before me" (Gen. 20:2). To affirm ultimate allegiance to God is to deny ultimate allegiance to any other god, whether the Baals of the Canaanite culture or the god of a particular tribe, nation, ideology, or political party. If there is a conflict between what God demands, and what any other god demands, the choice is clear. One says "yes" to the demand of God and in that act simultaneously says "no" to the demand of the other god.

The theme is picked up by the Christian community. When ordered to stop preaching, Peter replies with a phrase that is the charter for a counter-culture: "We must obey God rather than men" (Acts 5:29). If there is a conflict between the demand that God makes (in this case to preach the good news) and the demand that the culture makes (in this case to stop preaching), the conclusion is unavoidable: "We must obey God."

[6] For fuller development of the ensuing points, cf. R. M. Brown, *The Pseudonyms of God* (Philadelphia: Westminster Press, 1972), especially Part III.

The earliest Christian creed consisted of two words: *Kurios Christos* (Christ is Lord). This was as political as it was theological, for the Roman Empire demanded a contrary affirmation, *Kurios Caesar* (Caesar, the State, is Lord). Thus to say that "Christ is Lord" was to affirm not only a different drum beat but even to identify the drummer.

When the King of England demanded of Thomas More a measure of loyalty that seemed to More to invalidate the demands of conscience and the demands of God, More demurred. The King then asked More whether or not he was the King's good servant. More replied, in another formulation of the counter-culture position, "I am, Sire, the King's good servant, but I am God's good servant first."

With the rise of Nazism in Germany, the various institutions of German society capitulated to Hitler—the army, the business community, the university, most of the church. But a few within the church did not. They formed the Confessing Church, recognizing that to give Hitler the unqualified allegiance he demanded was (to recapitulate our previous examples) to disobey the first commandment, to obey men rather than God, to say "Caesar is Lord," and to be the State's good servant first. It was out of the clarity of their affirmation that their negations came, in the Barmen Confession of 1934, in which they stated that in the light of commitment to Jesus Christ they could not acknowledge the authority of other "events and powers," nor could they allow areas of their life to be ruled by other than him.

Each of the above examples communicates the disturbing fact that a price was paid for the counter-culture stance. The Jews have paid the price of centuries of persecution, members of the early church faced crucifixion and the lions, Thomas More was beheaded, members of the Confessing Church were hanged. A culture is always threatened by those who challenge its values, but a church that is unwilling to face the likelihood of such threats is not a church that deserves to survive.

A Catholic image with a Protestant twist: "Christian presence"

In the midst of World War II, a disturbing analysis by Abbé Godin, a French Roman Catholic priest, in the book *France:*

Pays de Mission?, inspired Cardinal Suhard of Paris to move
in a new direction. Up to that time priests had lived in se-
cluded rectories next to almost empty churches, wearing cassocks that set them apart from ordinary folk and tending to a
dwindling number of the elderly. The rank and file cared little
about the church. Cardinal Suhard was convinced by Abbé
Godin's argument that France was no longer a "Catholic country," but a missionary country, and reasoned that "since the
people are not coming to church, the church must go to the
people." He therefore released a number of priests from their
cassocks and rectories so that they could wear ordinary working clothes, rent flats in tenement areas, and take factory jobs.
The movement of the worker-priests (*les prêtres-ouvriers*) was
born.[7]

Once the initial suspicions had been overcome, many of the
priests were elected to positions in labor unions. Their flats
became places of social gathering and labor organizing. Their
kitchen tables became places around which a simple eucharist
was celebrated. After several years, one of the worker-priests
was asked what he had "accomplished": Had many people
come back into the church? Was the influence of the church
being restored? His description of what had been "accomplished" was merely, *C'est la présence, c'est la présence!* which
we might translate, "What matters is simply being there."

This is not the place to recount the subsequent difficulties of
the worker-priest movement, which fell afoul of the Vatican
and was virtually dead for a decade before gaining a new lease
on life after Vatican II. But it is the place to point out that the
image of "Christian presence" is an important image for the
frontier life of the church today.

The Catholic image, however, needs a Protestant twist, a
twist that most Catholics would now be willing to accept. Implicit in Cardinal Suhard's approach was the assumption that
"the church" equaled "the clergy" and that the church was
present in the world once the clergy were present in the world.
It has always been a Protestant contention, however, that "the
church" equals "the whole people of God" and that clergy cannot act as surrogate for laity. If we take Christian presence

[7] Cf. M. Ward, *France Pagan?* (New York: Sheed and Ward, 1949),
for the story of Abbé Godin and the text of his book, and *The Worker-
Priests* (London: Routledge and Keegan Paul, 1956), for documents
about the movement itself.

seriously, it must involve all church members and not only those set apart by ordination. This will mean church members being there (*la présence*), wherever there is need, not for overt proselytizing but simply because there is a need to be met that no one else is meeting. It does not mean that Christians must hide their light under a bushel; when asked to give an accounting of their presence, they will surely do so, but they will be released from feeling that a verbal accounting of the faith is their top priority. Christian presence will be embodied through deed more than through word.

Those who feel that this represents an ecclesiastical copout, need to be reminded that the hollowness of much Christian rhetoric today has been exposed and that the gap between proclamation and performance has been stretched to the breaking point. It is patently clear, for example, that the American Christian community has been long on pronouncements about peace and short on opposition to war, which would seem to be a logical place to tackle the problem of world peace. Whatever concern has been communicated has been more through what churches have done than through what they have said; churches that have offered symbolic "sanctuary" to draft resisters, for example, have been a more creative Christian presence through the act of physical and moral identification with young men of conscience, than have those churches that talked in impeccably orthodox tones about Jesus Christ as an individual savior and turned their backs on those who found such terminology unconvincing.

The real communication of Christian presence will come as Christian groups—congregations, synods, denominations—invest both their human and financial resources in ghetto programs, combine forces with secular groups working against racial discrimination, sponsor low-cost housing, and release members from Sunday school teaching to lobby against the arms race. "At this moment in the world's history," the black author James Baldwin told the delegates at the World Council of Churches Assembly in 1968, "it becomes necessary for me, for my own survival, not to listen to what you say, but to watch very carefully what you do." Communication through deed is the essence of Christian presence. The word is commentary on the deed, not the other way around.

But there is a problem with Christian presence. It represents a creative response to the present, but it could become a destructive response to the future. Unless Christian presence does persuade some persons to pass on the faith through an ongoing community, in a short time there will be no community left to pass it on. As we saw in Chapter 6, it is false to assume that the church needs no institutional embodiment. And even though the number of Christians who band together may significantly diminish, it is surely counter-productive to anticipate that it might dwindle to zero.

The church as we know it today may actually have to endure death before it can experience resurrection. This observation is theologically sound if coupled with the understanding that a remnant is on hand as a continuation between the two events. The earliest disciples lived through the period from Good Friday to Easter; had they not, there would have been no one on hand to recognize the risen Lord.

This says some things about the inner life of the church during the travail of death and resurrection into which we may be entering. The theme of Christian presence must be embraced within the dialectic of summoning and sending. As Christians are present in the world they will also need to be present to one another, in ways that as yet are far from clear. Dietrich Bonhoeffer probed this as few of our contemporaries have done, but his comments are fragmentary and elusive, centering around what he called "the secret discipline" and the importance of maintaining the life of prayer and action whether such discipline "communicated" to the outside world or not. Whatever else he may have meant by secret discipline, Bonhoeffer saw that in the midst of change there must also be some thread of continuity, a lifeline to the best that had come before, so that when once again the old words could speak with new power (or new words had been found to communicate the old power), the heritage would not have been lost.[8]

A Protestant image with a Catholic twist: The "pilgrim people"

One of the most striking facts about contemporary life is its mobility. Not only do people travel thousands of miles in a few

[8] One of the fullest discussions of the secret discipline is contained in A. Dumas, *Dietrich Bonhoeffer: Theologian of Reality* (New York: Macmillan, 1972), Chapter VII, especially pp. 197–214.

hours, but they change their place of dwelling with astonishing frequency; in the United States alone, one out of every five persons moves each year. People are "on the march," *in via*, once more "strangers and pilgrims on the earth."

There is a difference, however, between a pilgrimage planned to fulfill a lifelong goal and a trip or a tour undertaken for momentary diversion. Also, the young executive who is suddenly moved from Pittsfield to Omaha does not necessarily view the move as bringing him closer to his final destination, and he may resent the uprooting of his family. He may not even have a clear picture of what his final destination is, and confusion rather than direction may therefore characterize his life. Being on the march may define a destructive rather than a creative way of life.[9]

Nevertheless, when such cautions have been noted, the theme of mobility is a helpful *entré* into the imagery of the church as a people on the march, engaged in a pilgrim existence.

In the polemical situation of the Reformation, Christians became polarized in their images of the church, Protestants stressing the entire "people of God," and Catholics stressing the hierarchical structure to which the rest were subordinate. However, the Protestant stress on the entire people has recently been re-affirmed in Catholic thinking in a way that draws both groups closer, and they converge in the image of the pilgrim people. Both the noun and the adjective are important.

The noun stresses the basic truth that the church is the whole people of God. "The priesthood of all believers" has been a way of insisting that all Christians share in ministry and that ordained ministers are those set apart chiefly to help the laity be better ministers, as well as to perform certain functions (such as the administration of the sacraments) so that all things may be done "decently and in order." The new Catholic recognition of this emphasis is symbolized by a shift in the order of the chapters of the document on the Church at Vatican II. The original order represented a traditional approach:

Chapter 1—The Mystery of the Church
Chapter 2—The Hierarchy
Chapter 3—The People of God

[9] Cf. further on these points W. Kuhns, *op. cit.*, pp. 97–99.

However, in the final draft the order was shifted:

> Chapter 1—The Mystery of the Church
> Chapter 2—The People of God
> Chapter 3—The Hierarchy

Thus it was acknowledged that the basic description of the church is the whole people of God and that only when that is clear can one talk about the hierarchy as a part of the whole people.

Recent Protestant discussion has acknowledged that the basic ministry is the ministry of all the people by suggesting that baptism (entering the church) is really ordination (being set apart to minister) and that any special ministry to which one might be set apart is in the context of a ministry that all share by virtue of their baptism.

But the image of the people of God could be static without the adjective. The people are a pilgrim people. The crucial point, the safeguard against complacency or pride, is the recognition that the people of God have not arrived. They are still on the way. New forms, new patterns, new emphases will be necessary, so that the church can experiment and avoid getting locked into past forms, patterns, and emphases. John Mackay has commented:

> The whole Church must brace itself to face the frontier. That is to say, it must become a mobile missionary force ready for a wilderness life. It must be ready to march toward the places where the real issues are and where the most crucial decisions must be made. *It is a time for us all to be thinking of campaign tents rather than of cathedrals.*[10]

The provisional nature of present church forms is clearly elucidated in the report of the 1961 assembly of the World Council of Churches at New Delhi:

> A reappraisal of the patterns of church organization and institutions inherited by the younger churches must be attempted, so that outdated forms which belonged to an era that is rapidly passing away may be replaced by strong

[10] In C. Ranson, ed., *Renewal and Advance* (London: Edinburgh House Press, 1948); italics added.

and relevant ways of evangelism. This is only one illustration, but an important one, of how the Church may become the Pilgrim Church, which goes forth boldly as Abraham did into the unknown future, not afraid to leave behind the securities of its conventional structures, *glad to dwell in the tent of perpetual adaptation,* looking to the city whose builder and maker is God.[11]

The imagery of the tent is a useful way to contemplate the meaning of the pilgrim people. Anton Henze has suggested that the architecture of each stage of Christian history reflects a certain notion of the church and the culture surrounding it.[12] Around A.D. 400, the typical church was the basilica, reflecting the halls of justice and commerce of the time. At the height of its medieval imperial and ecclesiastical power, the cathedral was strong and mighty, a castle or fortress. In an age such as ours, in which man has become rootless and homeless, some church architects have attempted to communicate the feeling of the tent. The notion is admittedly difficult to capture in stone and steel, but Henze feels that such a design as that of Fritz Metzger's Church of SS. Felix and Regula in Zurich is a step in this direction.[13]

In addition to stressing adaptability and mobility, the image of pilgrim people suggests one further theme: the ongoing reformation of the church. The relationship between pilgrimage and ongoing reformation was clearly recognized by Vatican II:

> Christ summons the church as she goes her pilgrim way, to that continual reformation of which she always has need, insofar as she is an institution of men here on earth.[14]

Since the church is incomplete and unfinished, it will always be in need of divine forgiveness, and must always hope for the purging and judgment and renewal that are necessary to an

---

[11] W. A. Visser 't Hooft, ed., *The New Delhi Report* (New York: Association Press, 1962), p. 90, italics added to call attention to one of the greatest phrases in ecumenical literature.

[12] Cf. A. Henze, *Contemporary Church Art* (New York: Sheed and Ward, 1956).

[13] I have elaborated these themes in "True and False Witness: Church Architecture Today," *Theology Today* (January, 1967), pp. 521–37.

[14] W. M. Abbot, ed., "On Ecumenism," *Documents of Vatican II* (New York: Associated Press, 1966), p. 350.

institution *in via*. The fullness of the church is not present during a time of pilgrimage, and a pilgrim people must recognize day after day that "judgment must begin at the house of God." This recognition that the church has not yet arrived provides that margin for judgment without which the church's claims for itself could become pretentious.

A contemporary political image: "The movement"

One of the most important and elusive images on the contemporary scene is the collection of individuals, splinter groups, and strange ideological bedfellows usually referred to as "the movement." It is a constantly shifting, frequently bickering, sometimes highly effective coalition of various interests. Richard Neuhaus describes its extraordinary span of diverse interests:

> It is a mass movement of revulsion against mindless slaughter in Vietnam. It is an elitist movement of political *illuminati* who refine the theories of class warfare. It is a black movement of isolation to build identity and resources for blackness in power rather than dependence. It is a black movement of alliance with any color or nationality prepared to join in overthrowing capitalist imperialism. It is a black movement of militant faith that the promise of the American Experiment can be invoked for the liberation of black and white alike. It is a youth movement in search of community and personal meaning beyond consumption and technology. It is a youth movement in resistance to hypocrisy and fear, to the gift of a poisoned heritage which they did not ask for and do not want. It is also a middle-aged movement of discarded dreams retrieved.[15]

What will happen to the movement? It may collapse from its own internal differences; it may coalesce into a new political party; it may remain as a gadfly, buzzing and annoying the establishment in unpredictable ways; it may be co-opted by the very institutions it seeks to transform. What is clear is that if the movement becomes too structured, it will cease to be a

[15] P. L. Berger and R. J. Neuhaus, *Movement and Revolution* (New York: Doubleday-Anchor, 1970), p. 89.

movement and become something else—a party, a church, an organization. Whatever else it gains by becoming one of the latter, it will lose some of the mobility, spontaneity, and freshness that characterizes its origins.

What does this mean for the church? There is no special virtue in the diffuseness and bickering that characterize the movement. But there is great virtue in the mobility, spontaneity, and freshness that it has generated on the American scene, and these are precisely the qualities needed in the church today.

The irony of the situation is that the church itself started out as a movement. It was a heterogeneous collection of fishermen, tax collectors, Jews, Gentiles (after a few early battles to keep them out), prostitutes, tentmakers, slaves, and widows. For several hundred years they had no buildings, no seminaries. As we have seen in earlier chapters, official recognition gave the movement respectability, leading to higher degrees of organization, coupled with less mobility, spontaneity, and freshness.

We are living in a time when the organizational and structural accumulation of the centuries has become a liability rather than an asset, a time when (as we have seen) there is a new imperative to travel light and recover some of the long-lost mobility, spontaneity, and freshness that once characterized the church. We need to embrace the image of the movement as a viable and necessary image for the church today.

An initial step in this direction has been taken by Father Gregory Baum, who has applied the phenomenon of the movement today to his thinking about the church of tomorrow.[16] He distinguishes between inner-oriented movements, such as Alcoholics Anonymous, whose purpose is to transform the individual, and outer-oriented movements, whose purpose is to transform the society of which they are a part. The latter (to which he wishes to compare the church) naturally have an effect on their own members, but the wider aim is to influence the entire human community. An "open church" (a term

---

[16] Cf. G. Baum, *The Credibility of the Church Today* (New York: Herder and Herder, 1968). Father Baum's analysis differs from the above in that he sees the movement as primarily a sociological rather than a political image. With this qualification, however, his comments are helpful to the present discussion.

Father Baum appropriates from Michael Novak) will not be defined in terms intrinsic to itself but "must be defined in terms of the whole human race and of its role in it." [17] The aim of the movement is not to become co-extensive with society, but to be an outer-oriented movement in society.

An outer-oriented movement is further characterized, Father Baum continues, by the fact that there are many ways of belonging to it. It does not have a clearly defined membership, and different people are involved in different ways. The boundary lines are not visible and precise. This was not a characteristic of the church in the past—one was either "in" or "out"—but it must be a characteristic of the church in the future. In terms of a distinction developed in Chapter 6, there is no equivalence between the Kingdom of God and the institutional structure we call the church. One can be passionately committed to the former and yet take his membership in the latter with a grain of salt. He can be what François Roustang calls *le troisiéme homme,* the third man who is neither "progressive" nor "conservative," who is deeply committed to the Christian tradition and sees the church as his spiritual home, but who is not going to spend all his time fighting intramural battles.

Another characteristic of an outer-oriented movement is that it is "institutionally visible at the centre." [18] It can be discerned at work when meetings are held, committees are functioning, and rallies are taking place, but its outer boundaries cannot be clearly drawn. Its greatest contribution to those around it will probably not come from its meetings, committees, and rallies, but when those within it are engaged in the exercise of its mission. This does not mean that it will have no structures, but that its members (and non-members) will not measure the presence and reality of the movement by the visibility and outward efficiency of its organizational life.

When these characteristics are put together it is possible to make any number of projections about how the image of the movement could be applied to new ways of ordering the life of the church. Such projections should never be taken as blueprints, for what is useful in one situation may be inadequate in another. Father Baum offers one such projection:

[17] *Ibid.,* p. 197 ff.
[18] *Ibid.,* p. 105.

Let us assume that a large North American city has 40 parishes. Parish means closed society. A parish has geographical boundaries. The pastor is in charge of the parish; he is appointed over the people. Then let us imagine that instead of these 40 parishes we have 10 or 15 centres of Christian life, conveniently spread over the whole city, without any territorial rights. At these centres, worship is celebrated on Sundays and throughout the week. Every day there are activities of various kinds in which people can involve themselves. There are talks, discussion groups, action programmes, adult education, catechesis for children . . . the action at the centres can be shared in by people. It stimulates them, makes them ask important questions, impresses on them the meaning of faith, and encourages them to reach out for the answers to new questions. People involve themselves in what happens at these centres, as they choose. When they go there no one has authority over them. If they want to participate on the organizational level, they will be able to do so, and eventually influence the making of policy regarding the centre. But what counts is not so much what happens at the centre but what happens in people's lives as the result of their contact with these centres.[19]

The value of this image is that it is open to new situations as they arise. And if there is one thing about which we can be sure in the decades ahead, it is that new situations will arise.

A concluding musical image: The *cantus firmus*

As we seek an image to draw our discussion together, it becomes clear that such an image is provided in the later prison writings of Dietrich Bonhoeffer.[20] To understand the full measure of what he is saying, it is important to understand the context in which he is writing. His friend and correspondent, Eberhard Bethge, who is serving with the German army on the Italian

[19] *Ibid.*, p. 207.
[20] Cf. D. Bonhoeffer, *Letters and Papers from Prison*, new, greatly enlarged edition (New York: Macmillan, 1972), especially pp. 303–305. Bethge's letters on pp. 283–84 provide the context for Bonhoeffer's response.

front, is disturbed at the way the priorities in his life have become disarranged. Bethge writes:

> Can you tell me anything about the fact that all my feeling and thinking is now really concentrated on personal experience, and that excitement over church affairs, love for its cause, has been caught up in a degree of stagnation? My conscious missionary impulse, which in earlier years was there perhaps more or less naively, has given way to the attempt to understand things, people and circumstances and to grasp them in a "human" way . . . .[21]

Later Bethge writes of the anxiety he feels in the face of bombing attacks by the Allies, made more devastating by the good weather, which rob him "of all composure."

Subsequently Bethge is granted home leave and visits Bonhoeffer in prison, where he talks of the anxieties he feels and the confusion arising out of the apparently conflicting loyalties between church, country, home and family, and survival. Bonhoeffer captures Bethge's mood in a letter written after the prison visit:

> I can't completely escape the feeling that there is a tension in you which you can't get rid of completely . . . . If a man loves, he wants to live, to live above all, and hates everything that represents a threat to his life. You hate the recollection of the last weeks, you hate the blue sky, because it reminds you of them, you hate the planes, etc. You want to live with Renate [Bethge's wife] and be happy, and you have a good right to that.[22]

Bethge's confusions and uncertainties are, in microcosm, the confusions and uncertainties of the church as well: What is a proper ordering of priorities? How can we discern and then affirm a sense of direction, stability, and hope? How can we sort out what is important from what is unimportant? In the midst of apparent chaos where can we find a base of assurance that is firm?

It is in relation to such questions that Bonhoeffer's musical image speaks not only to Bethge but to the church as well.

---

[21] *Ibid.*, p. 283.
[22] *Ibid.*, p. 302.

Drawing on his wide musical knowledge, Bonhoeffer first discusses "the polyphony of life," the wide variety of human experiences, analogous to the way a composer may keep three or four themes going simultaneously in a wild and apparently disjointed array of sounds. He then points out that what keeps the polyphony from being merely wild and disjointed is the *cantus firmus* (literally the fixed song), the ongoing plain chant or Gregorian melody that gives unity and meaning and direction to everything else. As long as the *cantus firmus* is clear and discernible, the polyphonic superstructure is not chaotic but is held together in an understandable and liberating way.

> There's always a danger in all strong, erotic love that one may lose what I might call the polyphony of life. What I mean is that God wants us to love him eternally with our whole hearts—not in such a way as to injure or weaken our earthly love, but to provide a kind of *cantus firmus* to which the other melodies of life provide the counterpoint. One of these contrapuntal themes (which have their own complete independence but are yet related to the *cantus firmus*) is earthly affection. Even in the Bible we have the Song of Songs; and really one can imagine no more ardent, passionate, sensual love than is portrayed there (see 7.6). It's a good thing that the book is in the Bible, in face of all those who believe that the restraint of passion is Christian (where is there such restraint in the Old Testament?). Where the *cantus firmus* is clear and plain, the counterpoint can be developed to its limits . . . . Do you see what I'm driving at? I wanted to tell you to have a good, clear *cantus firmus;* that is the only way to a full and perfect sound, when the counterpoint has a firm support and can't come adrift or get out of tune, while remaining a distinct whole in its own right. Only a polyphony of this kind can give life a wholeness and at the same time assure us that nothing calamitous can happen as long as the *cantus firmus* is kept going.[23]

At the risk of seeming to systematize a spontaneous outburst, let us see what Bonhoeffer is affirming about the relationship of the *cantus firmus* and the polyphony of life:
The two are interrelated: earthly affection and divine love

---

[23] *Ibid.*, p. 303. In the printed text, the word translated "lose" in line two is incorrectly printed "love."

are part of the same overarching whole. One must not deny one for the sake of the other.

The two also have a certain independence. (On another occasion Bonhoeffer noted that to think of God while embracing one's wife was at least "in bad taste.") One is entitled to explore and live to the full the polyphony of life.

The reason for the dialectic of interrelationship and independence is that when the *cantus firmus* is sure, the polyphony is liberated and not bound. It can go in fresh and creative directions. There is no fear that it will be lost, for the *cantus firmus* provides the framework within which it can be fully developed.

There is a further fact about the *cantus firmus* that Bonhoeffer does not mention in his letter but that is helpful in adapting the imagery to the life of the church. This is the fact that the *cantus firmus* was a "given" with which the composer worked. He did not himself create the basic theme that made his polyphonic composition possible, but drew it from the musical heritage of the past.

It should not be necessary to develop in detail the obvious implications of this imagery for the life of the church. The task of the church is to keep the *cantus firmus* clear and distinct, so that both inside and outside the church the polyphony of life can be lived, experienced, tested, and stretched. Out of this relationship of *cantus firmus* and polyphony, a new set of contrapuntal themes can be developed for our day, themes that the whole human family can use with excitement and courage, themes that would bring to the *cantus firmus* a new embroidery of richness and beauty, at the same time that the *cantus firmus* supplies to the polyphony the coherence and assurance that is needed to make life unified and whole. The church, then, in its very sounding of the *cantus firmus*—a message not created by it but given to it—will be making legitimate and even insisting upon the ongoing polyphony of life, the whole range of experiences that Bonhoeffer subsumes under "earthly affection."

A musical analogy provides a useful transition to a consideration of liturgy to focus our discussion, and it is to a brief consideration of this theme that we turn in the final chapter.

9

The Frontier of Liturgy
or
Pulling It All Together

There is beauty and there are the humiliated. Whatever difficulties the enterprise may present, I would like never to be unfaithful either to the one or to the other.
—Albert Camus, *Lyrical and Critical Essays,* pp. 169–170

Most of this book has been concerned with the humiliated rather than with beauty. For the particular era in which we live, this is a proper emphasis; those who are reasonably well-fed and reasonably comfortable most of the time, need to be reminded that it is not reasonable that the majority of the human family should be ill-fed and uncomfortable all of the time. We are not entitled to "worship the Lord in the beauty of holiness," or even to contemplate "the holiness of beauty," at the cost of ignoring the ugliness and destructiveness that result from human greed or indifference.

But one does not deal with the reality of the humiliated in a vacuum. One always operates within a framework or a context. It may be the context of white fear: "Give the natives just enough so that they will avoid challenging the system that gives us so much and them so little." It may be the context of aggrieved paternalism: "We've done so much for them . . . and they're not even grateful." It may be, in rare but precious moments, the context of genuine compassion: "We have abused this beautiful earth, and even more the peoples of this earth. We must therefore risk our privileged position to repair the harm we have done." Thus the holiness of beauty—the beauty not only of nature but of human nature—could be the context for new sensitivity to the plight of the humiliated.

Camus' contrast can be stated in other ways as well. For beauty we could read love, and for the humiliated we could read the victims of injustice, so the statement would go:

> There is love and there are the victims of injustice. Whatever difficulties the enterprise may present, I would like never to be unfaithful either to the one or the other.

Another might think mystery, rather than beauty, and politics, rather than the humiliated, so that the statement would go:

> There is mystery and there is politics. Whatever difficulties the enterprise may present, I would like never to be unfaithful either to the one or the other.

The contrast could be made in still another way:

> There is God and there are persons. Whatever difficulties the enterprise may present, I would like never to be unfaithful to the one or the other.

But no matter what words were used, the point would remain that the two can never finally be separated.

That they can never finally be separated is what liturgy is all about.

Leitourgia as "the peoples' work"

This is not the way we usually think of liturgy. Liturgy has come to mean the special activity that people perform in church. This narrowing of the term is a linguistic catastrophe, since it has led precisely to the kind of dichotomy that Camus strove, and that all Christians with him must strive, to avoid. A proper understanding of liturgy could avoid such a dichotomy and integrate all that we have been saying about frontiers for the church today.

Let us see how this is so. An interesting set of terms proposed for the International Missionary Conference in 1947 at Whitby has provided much material for subsequent discussion of the nature and mission of the church and provides a helpful backdrop for our discussion. The terms are *kerygma, koinonia,* and *diakonia.* We can describe them schematically in the following way:

Kerygma means proclamation, the church's announcement of the good news that the Kingdom of God has come. It is the declaration in faith that we make today of what God has done in the past.

Koinonia means community, the showing forth or manifesting of the nature of the Kingdom of God here and now. It is the embodiment in love of what God is doing in the present.

Diakonia means service, the instrument for widening the Kingdom of God that is yet to be. It is the extension in hope of what God will do in the future.

Thus, our terms can be described in various ways: they deal with past, present, and future; they embody faith, hope, and love; they picture the church as announcer, embodier, and enabler; they point to the Kingdom of God as past event, present reality, and future possibility.[1]

But there was to have been a fourth term on the Whitby agenda, a companion to the above three, and one that apparently got lost in the scheduling problems of the conference. This was the term *leitourgia,* and it is time (at least in a preliminary way) to complete the Whitby agenda and show how a proper understanding of *leitourgia* can elucidate the interrelationship of beauty and the humiliated and also the interrelationship of *kerygma, koinonia,* and *diakonia.*

Leitourgia, as we have already noted briefly, does not mean only what people do in church. A wider understanding is indicated by the root meaning of the word, which, like so many theological words, is a transliteration from the Greek. *Leitourgia* is derived from *laos,* meaning people or laity, and *ergos* meaning work. Thus, liturgy properly defined means "the people's work," or "the work people do" wherever they are. It has no special reference to religious work. We have therefore debased the coinage of *leitourgia* by thinking instinctively of genuflections, hymnody, and public prayers as the only types of work described by the word liturgical.

We must recover the wider initial usage of the word so that

---

[1] These interrelationships will be developed in more detail in my forthcoming book tentatively titled *Is Faith Obsolete?*

we can say quite comfortably that liturgy is fulfilling jury duty, playing centerfield in Candlestick Park, singing praise, washing diapers, visiting the sick, making love, designing buildings, reading Holy Scripture, checking footnotes, receiving communion, or filling out one's income tax form. Properly understood, therefore, liturgy becomes a way of describing the wholeness, the oneness, the indissolubility of all of life. If certain abuses of the concept of liturgy can be escapist (what Helmut Thielicke has called "the flight into busywork and liturgical artcraft"), a full appropriation of the meaning of liturgy can make life all of a piece. Jesus saw this clearly enough: "If, when you are bringing your gift to the altar, you suddenly remember that your brother has a grievance against you, leave your gift where it is before the altar. First go and make your peace with your brother, and only then come back and offer your gift." (Matt. 5:23-24, N.E.B.)

The interrelationship was clearly seen by Dietrich Bonhoeffer in the early 1930's in Nazi Germany, when the German church was trying to ignore what was going on outside its walls. "Only he who cries out for the Jews," Bonhoeffer said, "has the right to sing Gregorian chant." Only he who identifies with the humiliated, we might paraphrase Bonhoeffer today, has the right to sing "A Mighty Fortress is Our God." But the converse is also true: Gregorian chant can sustain one as he goes forth to cry out for the Jews, and Luther's hymn can embolden one to risk more for the humiliated than he might otherwise risk without the assurance given by words Luther wrote with a price upon his head:

> Let goods and kindred go
> This mortal life also.
> The body they may kill,
> God's truth abideth still,
> His Kingdom is forever.

So liturgy is a way of putting together what we often falsely separate as going on "inside" or "outside" the church.

Liturgy also puts together the tasks of the church as they were delineated by the Whitby conference: *kerygma, koinonia,* and *diakonia* (proclamation, community, and service). For liturgy is simply the enactment, the embodiment, of what those realities mean. The announcement, the proclamation (*kerygma*), of the good news of forgiveness is communicated through liturgy, whether it is the liturgical act of proclaiming the Assurance of Pardon, or the equally liturgical act of embracing one with whom there has been a bitter dispute. The fellowship of persons (*koinonia*) is communicated through liturgy, whether it is the liturgical act of sharing one loaf around the Lord's Table in one place, or the equally liturgical act of legislating to provide enough loaves on kitchen tables in every place. The life of service (*diakonia*) is communicated through liturgy, whether it is the liturgical act of offering one's money in church on Sunday morning or the equally liturgical act of offering oneself in an office building on Monday morning.

The sacraments as an expression of life's unity

The point is driven home vividly in the sacramental actions of the church. Without trying to develop a full "theology of the sacraments," and at the risk of seeming to ignore other dimensions of their meaning, let us highlight one point: the centrality of the sacraments in the life of the church flatly denies that life can be compartmentalized as sacred and secular or as beauty and the humiliated. For the sacraments show us that the most holy, sacred, spiritual moment in the life of the church is directly dependent upon and communicated through the most earthy, secular, mundane objects imaginable —water in the case of baptism, and food and drink in the case of the Lord's Supper. When the church wants to demonstrate most clearly the presence of Christ in its midst, it does not ask people to listen in rapt silence to ethereal music or gaze motionless at stained glass windows; it passes around food, it invites people to eat and drink. And the bread it offers them (no matter how disguised as communion wafers) is still bread—bread that stands for Christ's body, but bread that also undeniably stands for sowing and harvesting, tractors and baking ovens, teamsters' unions and trucking concerns, economics and politics. In other words, no matter how hard we try to keep "the world" outside the church—whether by thick walls that shut out the noise of Main Street, stained glass windows that obscure factory smoke stacks, or middle-class mores that insist that weekday people can only approach God in Sunday clothes—the world intrudes, in the form of bread, in the form of wine, in the form of water. God gives us the presence of his Son by means of these very ordinary things.

Thus—although language lamely makes the point—we can have the sacred only through the secular, and we can understand the secular only as something that can be a vehicle of the sacred. Or, to put the matter bluntly, those who "go to church" to escape the world and all its demands may get a rude shock. For the world will follow them right in and, through worldly bread, confront them with Christ. But those who then go "out of church" to escape Christ and all his demands may get an even ruder shock. For Christ will follow them right out and, as one who was "known to them in the breaking of the bread," render judgment on a world where men starve for lack of bread.

Here, too, the traffic goes both ways. If the secular is the means of communicating the sacred, then the sacred invests the secular with new meaning. If Christ became human, then humanity is precious; if the world is God's handiwork, then the world is to be affirmed; if matter is God's instrument, then matter is good; if there can be a "holy meal" around an altar, then no meal around a dining room table is really profane. The phrase just cited, that Christ "was known to them in the breaking of the bread," comes not from the minutes of a great eucharistic congress, or from an account of a service in a temple or cathedral, but from an account of a handful of people having supper together in a private house in Emmaus, celebrating their return home from a day's journey.

The need for celebration

Celebration, indeed, is another key to the matter. For all that we have been saying about liturgy and sacrament means that we live in a world with a potential we have barely begun to appreciate, a world that is not to be rejected or scorned, but a world that is to be affirmed and indeed affirmed joyfully. It is a world that we not only cannot ignore when we worship, but a world without which we cannot truly worship at all, since it provides us with the necessary vehicles for worship.

It is a world in which we can never believe that God is off in heaven somewhere else, but a world about which we can and must say "Holy, holy, holy is the Lord of Hosts: the whole earth is full of his glory" (Isaiah 6:3).[2]

To be sure, we have covered up that glory and that presence with demonic skill, so that for many—perhaps even for most today—earth seems a hell rather than a heaven. But the point is that it is not meant to be that way and that there are resources available for bringing about the necessary transformation. That there is always the possibility of transformation and that there are always resources for bringing it about means that the keynote in the life of the church must be celebration— celebration of new possibilities, celebration of the fact that past failures need not immobilize the church but can liberate it to move in new directions, and, most fundamentally, celebration of the belief that the future is not closed but open.

If this note is lacking in the life of the church then the weight of human need and anguish will be a crushing burden that can only destroy those who dare to face that burden with sensitivity. Christians have every right to be perplexed (as St. Paul noted clearly) but not (as he noted equally clearly) to be perplexed unto despair. Indeed, despair may be the cardinal sin that tempts the church in our time, because it suggests that there are no new possibilities, no new opportunities, no real tomorrows. Alongside of this perplexity, as a contrasting term that is finally a conquering term, must go celebration, the affirmation by the church of what the Jews learned in the midst of their travail, and what Christians must reaffirm as they move on to the new frontiers that confront the church today and tomorrow—the dazzling truth that "the mercies of God are fresh every morning." Secure in that conviction, we can affirm that no "dark night of the soul" can finally extinguish the coming dawn and that, while frontier life will often be exacting, it will also always be exciting.

[2] Even if it is pointed out that Isaiah had his vision in the "sacred" confines of the temple, it can be further pointed out that he had already attached it to a very "secular" piece of information, namely that it all took place "in the year of King Uzziah's death." It is as though one were to say today, "I had a vision of God when Harry Truman was in the White House." In neither case is a cause-effect relationship implied. . . .

Annotated Bibliography

Probably there has been as much ink spilled in recent years by those attempting to rethink the meaning of the church, as there was blood spilled in earlier centuries by those attempting to deny to churches other than their own the right to continued existence. Out of an extraordinary number of available titles, the ones mentioned below are among those that in the author's opinion are either destined to make more than ephemeral impact or have been important catalysts in the ongoing discussion.

Samplings of the current debate about the church

The ecumenical era is firmly entrenched so that careful distinctions between "Protestant" and "Catholic" approaches to the meaning of the church are less important than they once were. There is a certain advantage in emphasizing Roman Catholic questioning about the church since the issues of continuity vs. change, or tradition vs. adaptation, are easily recognizable. Protestants can draw their own conclusions about how such discussion illuminates their own landscape.

Robert Adolfs, former Prior of the Augustinian Priory at Eindhoven, Holland, began pressing the need for change even before Vatican II had concluded. *The Church Is Different* (New York: Harper & Row, 1966) (published in Dutch in 1964), raises many far-reaching questions about reform and renewal. Adolfs followed this with the even harder-hitting *The Grave of God* (New York: Harper & Row, 1967). Richard McBrien, *Do We Need the Church?* (New York: Harper & Row, 1969), indicates ways in which Roman Catholicism must go beyond the ecclesiological position adopted at Vatican II, and his later paperback, *Church: The Continuing Quest* (Paramus: Newman Press, 1970), is a helpful survey and critique of post-Vatican II thinking about the church. A Roman Catholic response to the theological and pastoral implications of secularization is offered in Eugene Bianchi, *Reconciliation: The Function of the Church* (New York: Sheed and Ward, 1969). John R. McKenzie has raised important issues for the church's understanding of itself in *Authority in the Church* (New York: Sheed and Ward, 1966). The fullest overall interpretive survey of what has been happening to Catholicism in the United States is David O'Brien's *The Renewal of American Catholicism* (New York: Oxford University Press, 1972).

The problem of "staying in or getting out" is posed most forcibly by Charles Davis, a British Roman Catholic theologian, who gives his reasons for adopting the latter alternative in *A Question of Conscience* (New York: Harper & Row, 1967). Gregory Baum offers a response and a rationale for "staying in" in *The Credibility of the Church Today* (New York: Herder and Herder, 1968).

Hans Küng has posed immediate issues in such deliberately provocative volumes as *Truthfulness: The Future of the Church* (New York: Sheed and Ward, 1968); *Infallible? An Inquiry* (Garden City: Doubleday, 1971); and *Why Priests? A Proposal for a New Church Ministry* (Garden City: Doubleday, 1972).

The thrust toward new forms of church life is presaged in a symposium by both Protestant and Catholic churchmen, edited by Malcolm Boyd, *The Underground Church* (New York: Sheed and Ward, 1968), whereas Lewis Mudge, in *The Crumbling Walls* (Philadelphia: Westminster, 1970), offers a careful and informative account of new forms of church life and the ways in which they are breaking down ecumenical barriers.

Books typical of the ferment on the Protestant scene are the following, listed in roughly chronological order: J. C. Hoekendijk, *The Church Inside Out* (Philadelphia: Westminster, 1966); Albert van den Heuvel, *The Humiliation of the Church* (Philadelphia: Westminster Press, 1966); H. J. Schultz, *Conversion to the World* (New York: Scribners, 1967); John P. Brown, *Planet on Strike* (New York: Seabury Press, 1970); Roger Huber, *No Middle Ground* (Nashville: Abingdon Press, 1971); Robert Hudnut, *The Sleeping Giant: Arousing Church Power in America* (New York: Harper & Row, 1971). Much of the ferment has been aroused by such pioneering works as George Webber's *God's Colony in Man's World* (Nashville: Abingdon, 1960) and *The Congregation in Mission* (Nashville: Abingdon, 1964).

The problems, perils, and possibilities of church union, as mirrored in the Consultation on Church Union proposals among

ten denominations, are explored in detail from a great variety
of viewpoints in Paul A. Crow, Jr., and William J. Boney, eds.,
Church Union at Midpoint (New York: Association Press, 1972).

Major theological treatments of the doctrine of the church

While much of the current debate about the church is de-
signedly ephemeral, a kind of high-level pamphleteering meant
simply to carry the discussion one step further, there are a
number of relatively recent works that clearly will last and of
which account must be taken in subsequent discussions.

The most substantial works from the Roman Catholic side
have been Hans Küng, *Structures of the Church* (New York:
Thomas Nelson, 1964) and, even more important, his *The
Church* (New York: Sheed and Ward, 1967). These deal with
all the major historical and doctrinal questions, both for
Roman Catholics and for the Protestant-Catholic debate about
the church, and are extremely well decumented. Karl Rahner
deals with the doctrine of the church in many of his writings,
though essays on this topic are not all systematically gathered
together in one place. Places to begin are Rahner, *Theological
Investigations*, Vol. II (Baltimore: Helicon Press, 1963), on
the theme of "Man in the Church"; Vol, IV, which has four
essays on the sacraments; and Vol. VI, particularly Part IV on
"Contributions to a Theology of the Church." Careful analyses
of the various portions of the Vatican II constitution on the
church are contained in Herbert Vorgrimler, ed., *Commentary
on the Documents of Vatican II*, Vol. I (New York: Herder
and Herder, 1967).

One of the fullest recent Protestant treatments is in Karl
Barth, *Church Dogmatics* (Edinburgh: T. and T. Clark, 1956–
69), in the five "part-volumes" that comprise Vol. IV. Cf. IV/1,
para. 62 on "The Holy Spirit and the Gathering of the Christian
Community"; IV/2, para. 67 on "The Holy Spirit and the Upbuilding of the Christian Community"; IV/3, second half, para.
72 on "The Holy Spirit and the Sending of the Christian Community"; and IV/4 fragment, "The Foundation of the Christian
Life," dealing with baptism. Barth's emphases are indicated
by the shifting word in each of the three major paragraphs
above: gathering, upbuilding, and sending. The other major

Protestant treatment is Paul Tillich, *Systematic Theology*, Vol. III (Chicago: University of Chicago Press, 1963), especially Part IV, the sections on "The Manifestation of the Spiritual Presence in Historical Mankind" and "The Divine Spirit and the Ambiguities of Life," and Part V, the sections on "The Kingdom of God and the Churches" and "The Kingdom of God and World History."

The ecumenical scene

A full annotated ecumenical bibliography is included in Brown, *The Ecumenical Revolution*, revised and expanded edition (Garden City: Doubleday-Anchor Books, 1969), to which reference can be made for ecumenical writings up to 1969. Since then, "ecumenical writings" tend not to be writings *about* ecumenism per se, but writings about all sorts of subjects, done from an ecumenical perspective. This is a clear gain, not only to compilers of bibliographies but to the deepening of ecumenical insight.

Two important World Council of Churches studies, however, deserve special mention. The first of these is *The Church for Others*, consisting of two reports on "the missionary structure of the congregation" prepared by ecumenical working groups meeting over a period of several years. The second is Thomas Wieser, ed., *Planning for Mission*, which is a collection of working papers for the above noted study. Both are available from the World Council of Churches, Geneva.

The revolutionary frontier

Roland Bainton, *Christian Attitudes to War and Peace* (Nashville: Abingdon, 1960), is the fullest historical treatment of pacifism, the crusade and the "just war." S.G.F. Brandon, *Jesus and the Zealots* (New York: Scribners, 1967), puts Jesus very close to the revolutionary Zealot movement, a thesis that is disputed by Oscar Cullman in *Jesus and the Revolutionaries* (New York: Harper & Row, 1972) and by George Edwards in *Jesus and the Politics of Violence* (New York: Harper & Row, 1972). A well-documented book from a pacifist perspective is

John Yoder, *The Politics of Jesus* (Grand Rapids: Eerdmans, 1972).

The development of a "theology of development" can be traced in a number of documents issued by the World Council of Churches and the Commission on Society, Development and Peace (SODEPAX), both located in Geneva. The subject is clearly launched in P. Abrecht and M. M. Thomas, eds., *World Conference on Church and Society* (Geneva: World Council of Churches, 1967), the official report of the 1966 Geneva Conference on "Christians in the Technical and Social Revolutions of our Time," and is continued in *World Development: Challenge to the Churches*, the official report of the Conference on World Cooperation for Development, held at Beirut in 1968, and sponsored by the World Council of Churches and the Pontifical Commission on Justice and Peace. Most of the recommendations of the conferences were officially adopted by the fourth world assembly of the World Council of Churches in 1968, texts of which are available in N. Goodall, ed., *The Uppsala Report* 1968 (Geneva: World Council of Churches, 1968). *Peace—The Desperate Imperative* (Geneva, 1970), the report of a SODEPAX Conference on "Christian Concern for Peace," is a good summary of subsequent reflection on the problem. An exhaustive bibliography is available in G. Bauer, ed., *Towards a Theology of Development* (Geneva: SODEPAX, 1970), listing over 2000 items.

Challenges to a "theology of development" have been coming from representatives of third world countries, who are proposing that it be replaced by a "theology of liberation." The best pointers to this new position are the Peruvian Bishops' Commission for Social Action, *Between Honesty and Hope* (Maryknoll: Orbis Books, 1970), a collection of papers and essays from Latin America with special attention to the important Medellín Conference in 1968, and Gustavo Guitierrez, *A Theology of Liberation* (Maryknoll: Orbis Books, 1972), a substantial and original contribution which also has exhaustive documentation. Arend van Leeuwen, *Development Through Revolution* (New York: Scribners, 1970), describes further reasons for the shift.

A fuller treatment of materials on the church and the political revolutions of our time is contained in the annotated bibliography in my *Religion and Violence* (Philadelphia: Westminster, 1973).

The technological frontier

In the area of the technological revolution a large body of literature has developed in a relatively short space of time, ranging all the way from analyzing the merits and faults of a computer culture to pushing the panic button on the ecological crisis.

William Kuhns has opened up many issues for the nonspecialist in *Environmental Man* (New York: Harper & Row, 1969) and *The Post-Industrial Prophets* (New York: Weybright and Talley, 1971). A basic work, constantly referred to in the subsequent literature is Thomas Kuhn's *The Structure of Scientific Revolutions* (Chicago: University of Chicago Press, 1962); also available in later revised editions. Three useful overall surveys, dealing with a range of problems in some detail and containing helpful annotation and bibliography are Victor Ferkiss, *Technological Man: The Myth and the Reality* (New York: New American Library, 1969); John McHale, *The Future of the Future* (New York: Ballantine Books, 1971); and Emmanuel Mesthene, *Technological Change: Its Impact on Man and Society* (New York: New American Library, 1971).

Individual books from a variety of viewpoints that have had considerable influence on the discussion are Jacques Ellul, *The Technological Society* (New York: Knopf, 1964), which is a pessimistic analysis of our enslavement to the machine; R. Buckminster Fuller, *Operating Manual for Spaceship Earth* (New York: Simon and Shuster, 1969), which has a much more hopeful outlook; Marshall McLuhan, *The Medium Is The Message* (New York: Bantam Books, 1967), which is always catching the reader off guard; and Norbert Weiner, *The Human Use of Human Beings* (Garden City: Doubleday-Anchor Books, 1954), which deals with the interaction of man and machine. A recent popular survey in a popular style of prospects for the subsequent culture emerging in a technological era is Alvin Toffler's *Future Shock* (New York: Random House, 1970).

A number of theologians are beginning to examine the

theological implications of technology. Ian Barbour, *Science and Secularity* (New York: Harper & Row, 1970), discusses the ethics of technology, and a symposium under his editorship, *Earth Might Be Fair* (Englewood Cliffs: Prentice-Hall, 1972), explores issues of ecology. Harold Hatt, *Cybernetics and the Image of Man* (Nashville: Abingdon, 1968), is "a study of freedom and responsibility in man and machine." Arend van Leeuwen, *Prophecy in a Technocratic Era* (New York: Scribners, 1968), deals with the approach of the church to the new world in which it finds itself.

Further treatment of images of the church

The basic work with which to pursue the theme of images is Paul Minear, *Images of the Church in the New Testament* (Philadelphia: Westminster, 1960). For a Roman Catholic perspective on some of the same themes, cf. Rudolf Schnackenburg, *The Church in the New Testament* (New York: Herder and Herder, 1965). In addition to references cited on the *diaspora* image in Chapter 7 above, a few further works can be noted. The imagery of "outside the camp" is further developed in Charles West, *Outside the Camp: The Christian and the World* (Garden City: Doubleday, 1959). Further materials on contemporary adaptation of the images of religious orders and the counter-culture are available in Rosemary Ruether, *The Church Against Itself* (New York: Herder and Herder, 1967) and *Liberation Theology* (New York: Paulist Press, 1973), especially Chapters 2 and 3. Many books treat the image of the servant church within an overall discussion; Lewis Mudge's *In His Service* (Philadelphia: Westminster, 1959) is a fuller approach, and basic to almost all later discussion are the elusive hints on the theme of "the church for others" in Dietrich Bonhoeffer's *Letters and Papers from Prison*, new and greatly enlarged edition (New York: Macmillan, 1972). On the theme of "Christian presence," in addition to John Petrie, translator, *The Worker Priests* (London: Routledge and Kegan, 1956), there is helpful material in J. M. Domenach and R. de Montvalon, eds., *The Catholic Avant-Garde: French Catholicism Since World War II* (New York: Holt, Rinehart and Winston, 1967), especially Part II, "A Mission Country," and Henri Perrin, *Priest and Worker* (New York: Holt, Rinehart and Winston, 1964), an autobiography by one of the most active proponents of the worker-priest movement.

On the theme of celebration developed in the final chapter, cf. Gabriel Fackre, *Humiliation and Celebration: Post-Radical Themes in Doctrine, Morals and Mission* (New York: Sheed and Ward, 1969). The approach to the sacraments developed in the same chapter is partly dependent on the literature of the Iona Community: cf. especially George Macleod, *Only One Way Left* (Glasgow: The Iona Community, n.d.) and Donald Baillie, *The Theology of the Sacraments* (New York: Scribners, 1957).

For a look at the freedom that new images of the church can provide, see the writings of Daniel Berrigan, who has written widely from a radical Catholic stance. Randomly, among many writings, *America Is Hard to Find* (Garden City: Doubleday, 1972) will communicate something of the spirit of a very free spirit.

Index of Proper Names

Index of Scripture References